Little Miss Little Compton

A MEMOIR

Arden Myrin

RUNNING PRESS

PHILADELPHIA

Running Press
Hachette Book Group
1290 Avenue of the Americas, New York, NY 10104
www.runningpress.com
@Running_Press

Printed in the United States of America

First Edition: September 2020

Published by Running Press, an imprint of Perseus Books, LLC, a subsidiary of Hachette Book Group, Inc. The Running Press name and logo is a trademark of the Hachette Book Group.

The Hachette Speakers Bureau provides a wide range of authors for speaking events. To find out more, go to www.hachettespeakersbureau.com or call (866) 376-6591.

The publisher is not responsible for websites (or their content) that are not owned by the publisher.

Photo Credits: Courtesy of Arden Myrin

Print book cover and interior design by Rachel Peckman.

Library of Congress Control Number: 2019957375

ISBNs: 978-0-7624-6957-4 (hardcover), 978-0-7624-6956-7 (ebook)

LSC-C

10 9 8 7 6 5 4 3 2 1

For My Sweet Mama Bear,
I love you and miss you so much.

All the world is made of faith, and trust, and pixie dust.

—**Peter Pan**

CONTENTS

FOREWORD

by Debby Ryan

When my friend and yours, Arden Myrin, asked me to write the foreword to her book, I cried in her passenger seat. And then we went and got tacos. Arden has told me so many wild stories from her life, each one more hilarious and bizarre than the last, that I figured I must have heard them all by now. Not true. This book is filled with even more new gems than I could have expected. If I didn't know Arden, I probably wouldn't believe a lot of what's in these pages. But it's too specific, too bananas, and too canonically Arden to be made up.

I've never known such a gorgeous tornado of a soul, with an even larger hurricane swirling in different forms around her life. I can't tell whether Arden has a distinctly funny perspective or she just attracts ridiculous things. I consider hangouts with Arden my Ab Day because the laughter is always sidesplitting. It's also a sort of therapy because the conversation is self-aware and challenges me to think about things in new ways.

I've spent a lot of time in Arden's passenger seat. Spending time with Arden really makes you start to see the funny in everything. In the time it takes to get to and from a shitty taco joint, we have usually started forty different conversations and finished four. We've been stared at by strangers and disturbed the peace; I've been blindsided by the iron fist of wisdom in the velvet glove of laughter. That's Arden. I'm excited this book exists so that you can get to know her as I have.

When I arranged a private twerkout class in a Hasidic rec center, I never could've imagined it would be the place where my friend would hear some of the worst news of her life. Arden and I had been getting closer, and in many ways she had scooped me into her passenger seat, and I've watched her follow her path.

That day, I got in the driver's seat and came to care about Arden on our trip to Grief Island in a way I'd never anticipated. Arden's sense of humor courses through her and is present in every way. The absurd nature of her personality lets you know why she is the way she is. I've been told that God doesn't waste pain, and I have seen firsthand the beauty and comedy Arden was able to find even during the shadows of tragedy.

Arden has taught me that it's okay to feel like you're way too much and not enough at the same time. She's taught me how to identify the things you come by honestly. She's held my hand and taught me to listen for the difference between my little monster voices and the ones that actually want to help me. She's showed me how to turn my damage into superpowers and take the control back from the unproductive things. (She didn't teach me not to date the drummer.)

I've learned, by watching Arden navigate heartbreak, that my biggest fear could come true, but that I could still put myself back together. I've learned about the power of holding my own and allowing myself to have a delayed reaction. I've seen the importance of play (of spending time with people who make me feel good) and tacos.

Arden's mom, JJ, whom you'll come to know through Arden's book, nicknamed me The Pistol. And pistol see pistol. You see, the special thing about the difficult timing of this story is that you can find fingerprints from JJ's jazz hands in the big lessons. You'll learn to protect your magic and to start building your own boat. You'll realize that if you look for them, you will see fireflies.

I hope you enjoy this book and love the journey. It's a whole riot; it's hard to believe and impossible to doubt. Go on the ride and don't be a drip.

INTRODUCTION

It all started with my grandparents, the founding members of the Hasty Decisions Club. On January 26, 1937, in Philadelphia, a young businessman named Lars Myrin met a woman named Helen Latta. He thought she was pretty and fun; she thought he was rich. One day later they got married in Elkton, Maryland, because you didn't need a blood test to get hitched in Maryland. Five kids and five grandchildren later, my grandparents were married until the day they died, so it kind of worked out.

My parents, Janet and Willy, not only joined the Hasty Decisions Club, they bumped it up a notch: they married on a dare, and they weren't even dating. It's as if some Rubenesque, nonmusical Keith Richards decided to play marital chicken with Doris Day with one-too-many rosés in her.

Willy Myrin met Janet Olsen when they were coworkers on Wall Street. Willy was a party boy—think John Belushi but not as healthy. He was the second of five children, the wild child who gave himself nicotine poisoning when he snuck behind a shed and smoked an entire pack of Camels Unfiltered—in the third grade.

The happy newlyweds.

Janet Olsen didn't stand a chance against that bad boy. The cute girl in the office on Wall Street, Janet wore white gloves to work and would take the Long Island Rail Road into Manhattan every day from her parents' *Leave It to Beaver*–style household in Queens. She was the adorable secretary with great gams whose boss would chase her around the desk every day, *Mad Men* style. A practical girl, Janet nonetheless enjoyed a party and was up for a good time. She found that and much more in Willy Myrin.

The dare came about one night when Janet and Willy were having a few too many cocktails with coworkers after a day at the office and were trying to figure out how to wrangle the maximum amount of vacation time out of their employer. All employees got two weeks off a year, but if you went on a honeymoon you got an extra two weeks. My father then did the kind of math that only a drunk accountant could come up with: he offered to marry my mom so they could get the full four-week vacation. He would pay for them to go to South America for a month, and then they would come back to the States and get the marriage annulled. Keep in mind, they had never even kissed or been on a date with each other. Double-dog dare.

I am not surprised that my dad got married on a dare, but I am totally stunned that Janet did. Why did she do it? No one could fully understand her reasoning, but I think it was a perfect storm of factors. Having recently been dumped by her college boyfriend, Janet's guard was down, and at twenty-two she was worried she was becoming an old maid. (Oh, how times have changed.)

Another unquantifiable thing was that my dad was wild and could be very fun. Let's be honest, it can be hard to resist a bad boy. It was also a snowy, magical New York City night. Janet took the leap. She accepted his dare. My parents couldn't find a Bible to swear on, so they swore on a cookbook. The next day, my mom called my dad and raised the ante. She told him she would do it, but that if they got married she didn't want to get their marriage annulled. Checkmate.

Six weeks later they married at a country club in Long Island, my mother borrowing the wedding dress from her best friend Arden (my namesake). At the wedding, Willy's brother Bertie tried to persuade my father to jump out the dormer window in the men's bathroom, that it wasn't too late to escape. But Willy stuck to his dare. White as a ghost and sweating buckets, he stumbled down the aisle. Janet officially became a Myrin—pronounced "Marine" as in "The Few, The Proud, The Marines," but without the honor or the duty. (It's a drunk, Swedish Viking name—don't ask me.)

Janet and Willy at the scene of the crime.

After they got back from a whirlwind honeymoon, Willy told Janet that he would only live in one of two places: Manhattan or Little Compton, Rhode Island, where he had spent summers as a kid. Janet rolled the dice and chose the road less traveled—Little Compton—which has nothing in common with the California Compton. While the California Compton has produced such cultural heavyweights as N.W.A, Kendrick Lamar, Dr. Dre, The Game, and the album and film *Straight Outta Compton*, Little Compton's most famous resident is Poe the Crow, a bird that was on house arrest for stealing people's mail.

In a tiny country farm town, there is a real live-and-let-live quality to life. In other words, you can get really weird and set up your own independent nation on your property and no one will even question it. That's how Janet and Willy made a home governed by their own unique set of rules for life.

One year later my brother, Alarik (no relation to the Visigoth Alaric), was born, followed by moi, three and a half years later. I was born in the middle of a blizzard. When Willy

came to meet me for the first time at the hospital (no dads in the delivery room for Janet Myrin!), he did not come bearing flowers. Instead, he came with what every good woman who has just pushed out a seven-pound, seven-ounce butterball turkey really craves—a twelve pack of Drake's Devil Dogs.

Janet and her ginger baby, yours truly.

Upon meeting me, Willy declared: "She's not a blonde, she's a redhead. I've never met a redheaded woman I trusted!"

And so began my wild ride with the Myrin family. Did my parents seem like an odd fit for each other? Sure, but my brother and I just figured they fell in love at work like many couples do. We didn't find out about the dare until it slipped out one day when we were teenagers.

My brother, having never had a girlfriend in his life, came home from his freshman year in college with his first lady— an "older woman" (she was twenty), who was a soprano with perfect pitch. She would wince when I sang, plugging her ears. (Didn't she realize that I was secretly Mariah Carey?) They would go off to camps where they would practice square dancing and learn to sing madrigals while men in tights played on the mandolin. Alarik was glassy eyed from having sex for the first time. Who was this witchy woman, and what had she done with my big brother? But her arrival was crucial to explaining a key part of who I was. She was chatting with my mother one day when we were all in the car.

"Janet, how did you and Willy get engaged?"

"Oh, it was stupid. We married on a dare."

And that's when it all came out. We'd had no idea.

My brother freaked. "I'm sorry. WHAT?!!?"

But to me, it was the moment of enlightenment. Ahhh . . . *that* explains everything! We didn't *live* like a normal family because we didn't start out like a normal family. I am the result of not one, but *two* hasty decisions. And it was those hasty decisions that were the foundation for a unique set of life rules that could only have come about when these two people went off the grid with their lifestyle choices.

Growing up in my house was fun, warm, and inspiring but also confusing. The one constant was that most conventional rules were ignored. Marital courtship, bedtime (we were a house filled with night prowlers who stayed up into the wee hours even when I was in the fifth grade), pants (my dad wore nothing but boxers), the food pyramid (he ate nothing but cake), social norms (my mom would take me and my brother to school at ten a.m. because she felt like it wasn't fair to her night owl offspring to make them get up so early), and so on.

While it was a wild tale, my unusual upbringing gave me a unique set of tools—my mom encouraged creativity, shooting for the stars, making things, and being scrappy. From my mom, I learned that if I stayed true to myself, protected what was unique about me, and worked hard enough, wonderful things would be in store. I wouldn't have the life I have today if I didn't have Janet Myrin for a mom. But from my dad, I felt as if something was fundamentally wrong with me, and it has taken me many years to believe that nothing could be further from the truth. I also lacked basic skills—things like how to have a healthy relationship or how to set a boundary. Both seemed like a foreign language that I did not speak.

On top of this, all these questions kept popping into my head. What does being an adult even mean? What do normal people *do* on Sunday afternoons? Do people really pick up their phone when it rings?? NO WAY. How do you date someone who actually lives in the same city as you do? (I've always preferred a sex-piration date when it came to romance—*Only in town for six days? Let's fall in love!*) Do people really wake up well rested at 7 a.m., ready to "take on the day," without hitting the snooze button thirteen times? Most important, how do you start to believe that you are enough? (Well, first, you've got to get out into the world and start exploring.)

You see, when you grow up in a farm town like Little Compton, Rhode Island, which boasts a general store, no stoplights, and back in the day (rumor had it) an illiterate chief of police, you either thrive by getting handy, learn how to build a barn and live off the land, or you retreat into a fantasy universe in which you are a sophisticated, elegant, foxy, comedy superstar, and then you get the hell out of there two minutes after you turn eighteen. As I am not to be trusted with a hammer and have no need for a barn, I went the latter route. Make no mistake: there was nothing wrong with my town (it is actually the most magical small town); it was just not New York City or Hollywood or London—or even Schenectady.

I had a few things working against me in the sophisticated, elegant, foxy, comedy superstar department: (1) I had a red bowl cut and looked like Barb from *Stranger Things* and (2) I had no connections in the comedy world beyond farmer Mike, who once told me that I was "a real wack-a-do." Thanks, Mike.

I moved to New York and then to Los Angeles and tried to set up my adult life. While my work life was going great, it quickly

Good thing the Demogorgon didn't eat me on the end of a diving board!

became very clear that I had *no clue* how to actually *have* an adult life. I had no idea how to navigate the ins and outs as a fully grown human with the parental road map I'd been given. I mean, I didn't even know my way around LA! Damn you, Thomas Guide![1]

As I brought joy and creativity to my work life, I went about learning how to tackle the personal side of adulthood myself. I studied people, I made mistakes, I asked a lot of questions, and in the end, I actually put together a functioning toolbox that has helped me navigate life, work, dating, and, much to my surprise, marrying someone.

Here is everything I wish my younger self knew, and how I came to know it, usually in some embarrassing, funny fashion. Let's face it: no one gets life tools without some humiliation. Maybe some of my foibles can help a gal or guy coming after me from making the same mistakes. Shout-out to Little Compton!! *Woot Woot!*

---

1. Believe it or not, there was once actually a thick, horrible book of maps to find your way around Los Angeles. It was about 7,000 pages long and consisted of a confusing series of grids, numbers, and letters. Needless to say, I did not make it very far.

Shake Your Moneymaker

Do you feel like the God of Genetics robbed you in the foxiness department? Do images of influencers running around the Mediterranean in bikinis make you feel bad about yourself? It's not about what Mother Nature gave you. It's about what you do with what you've got. Shake it, don't break it, honey!

At the age of five, I was not what I appeared. On the surface, I looked like Ron Weasley from *Harry Potter*. "What a nice young man!" people would often exclaim after meeting me at our general store. What little girl doesn't dream of being called a "nice young man" surrounded by dusty cans of creamed corn?

Well, the joke was on them! Beneath the surface of this "nice young man" beat the heart of a hot, down-and-dirty . . . stripper. I was like that girl in

No need for a bike helmet when you have a helmet of ginger hair.

the '80s movie *Angel*[2]—"High school honor student by day. Hollywood hooker by night." But in my case it was more like *Arden*—"Kindergartener by day. Exotic dancer by night."

Don't let the fact that you look like a male wizard stop your commitment to dancing nude in public. I stripped. A lot. I was unstoppable. Believe me, people tried. In fact, *everyone* tried. Except my dad. Not that Willy was one of those creepy, why-isn't-he-in-jail kind of dads; he just wasn't really paying much attention to his child-rearing duties. He really stuck to the idea that because my mom was the one who wanted me and my brother, we were *her* responsibility.

I think my obsession with stripping began out of boredom—and because I was surrounded by a sea of handsome women in wool plaid. Sure, those hardy ladies could clear twelve acres of brush with their bare hands, but where did the razzle-dazzle come in? I first saw a stripper type on TV. No, it wasn't on cable—our town didn't get cable until, like, two days ago.

My childhood was a hodgepodge of typical '80s movies and TV shows combined with films from the 1930s. We had a channel that played old movies, and I saw a black-and-white movie with the Ziegfeld Girls[3] in it. They were vaudevillian, they had gigantic fans made out of feathers, they only wore tassels, and they were *electric*!! How could ladies so glamorous exist?!! Why didn't my mom dress like that? Why didn't *everyone* dress like that? Why would anyone ever choose to wear corduroy and

---

2. Look it up! This movie EXISTED!! It was dirty, it was mainstream, and it was EVERYWHERE!!!

3. The Ziegfeld Girls were showgirls from the turn of the twentieth century who wore elaborate costumes. Even though it was the 1980s, I was watching TV with content created in 1932.

turtlenecks when you could show cleavage and wear hot pants made of sequins and fringe?

Clearly, it was my calling to bring the erotic arts to the locals. Little Compton, Rhode Island, *needed* me. My mom moved to the booming metropolis of Little Compton from New York so her kids could "learn to make their own fun." You don't have to tell me twice! You know what's fun? Wiggling around in your underpants is fun. You know what's not fun? Slacks. Just because no one—and I mean *no one*—was buying what I was selling didn't mean my confidence had been rattled. I was determined to be Gypsy Rose Lee[4] for the frightened, unpaying kindergarten set. If at first you don't succeed, strip, strip again!

I grew up in a world of boys—I had a brother, five male cousins, three families of fake cousins (who were the offspring of my parent's former coworkers, with three boys each), and only one measly girl cousin, who didn't count because she lived in Wyoming. That's fifteen boys and one Wyoming girl. *WTF??* The upshot of thirty tiny testicles was that as a burgeoning stripper I had a lot of victims to choose from. The downside is that I was pinned down countless times, had spit dripped down and sucked up near my face, was locked in closets with spiders thrown on me, and was forced to play *Star Wars* more times than I can count.

My favorite targets were my brother's friends. Who can blame me? A house full of pasty, tiny boys dressed as R2-D2 was too much for my young heart to bear. Sadly, I had a *lot* of competition. My skinny brother rocking his Coke-bottle

---

4. This was a popular stripper on whom the musical *Gypsy* was based, not to be confused with Gypsy Rose Blanchard, who murdered her Munchausen-syndrome-by-proxy mother.

glasses and his motley crew of droids would be in his room for what seemed like days on end with the blinds drawn, rolling their multi-sided dice, playing *Dungeons & Dragons*. When they did venture into the *D&D*-free zone, they could barely handle daylight, never mind appreciate the sight of my five-year-old body wiggling around in my lollipop pants. But oh, how I tried.

I would attempt to outwit them and greet them at the front door rocking my new moves. If they didn't see me coming, they couldn't run as fast.

"Greetings, Jason. Is that a new cape you're wearing? I see you brought your fanciest lightsaber. Perhaps you didn't notice I have no clothes on."

Nothing.

It was as if he had been greeted at the door by a chair. Which leads me to my most important tip on stripping: just because people don't want to see you with your clothes off doesn't mean that you shouldn't flaunt it anyway. Perseverance commands success! BUT ASK FIRST, YA FILTHY ANIMALS!!! GET PERMISSION!

This tiny, naked Ron Weasley waited for my brother's friends behind trees in our yard, near the town jungle gym, and outside the dugout at their little league. You never know when you are going to get the opportunity to free yourself from the confines of your clothing. If you feel moved to strip and wiggle, by all means, rock it! Who cares if your body's not perfect, desired, or developed? Big deal! My stripping knew no boundaries. I stripped on playgrounds, in kitchens, at the pinewood derby, at my brother's Webelos troop, and at school. I was like a nude guerilla artist.

I wish I could say taking my show on the road was a smash hit. Sadly, the usual reaction was puzzlement, disinterest, and fear. My outfits didn't help. With my boy's bowl cut from Tommy the barber on the top and my brother's hand-me-down Wranglers on the bottom, I didn't exactly have the razzle-dazzle of a Ziegfeld girl. I begged my mother to dress me like Trixie, the daughter of the school bus driver, who was allowed to wear hot pink disco dresses and high heels. In first grade. But oddly, Janet Myrin wouldn't budge. Prude.

If I couldn't improve my outfits, I could at least work on my moves! Convinced my lack of training was causing people to overlook my obvious natural born talent, I decided to follow the age-old adage: How do you dance nude at Carnegie Hall? Practice, practice, practice.

I needed to work on my craft. As there was no local pole-dancing class for children, I was forced to squeeze my way into a tap dancing class in the basement of the local Catholic church. I wasn't Catholic and hadn't been raised with any religion in my family, but clearly I was being called by some kind of higher power—it was fate! God wouldn't give me this gift if he couldn't help me deliver the goods, right?

What better place to learn to move sensually than in the pea green linoleum tiled, Pine-Sol scented, wood-paneled community room of a Catholic church, surrounded by children in pink leotards and thick beige tights? The class was run by a stern woman named Mrs. DeMello, who had the most amazing, thick Rhode Island accent. She would scream at us as we practiced our kick ball changes: "One, two, three, foe-wah! One, two, three, foe-wah! Get your bum-bums movin'!"

Oh, I got my bum-bum movin' all right, just not at the same time as my feet. I had a hard time counting out a beat. I didn't want to plan out my moves to a counted measure; I just wanted to be free. Don't rein me in! I thought of myself as a gyrating jazz artist, my pelvis being my instrument. I decided to let my freak flag fly. While the other girls were tapping away to "On the Good Ship Lollipop," I began moving, pumping, and grinding up and down the green linoleum of that basement—I was hot shit. One, two, pump, grind, three, wiggle, FOE-WAH! Get your crotch movin'! Oh my god, I was getting it!

Lost in reverie, I felt like I was actually helping Mrs. DeMello, that I was her unpaid apprentice. Surely even the sternest Rhode Islander could recognize something special in me and that something divine was moving through my body. I heard my name being called.

"Ah-den! Ah-den!"

Was she cheering me on?

"Cool yo-ah jets, Ah-den! Do I have ta call yo-ah mutha?!"

No, she was not cheering. Apparently, my freestyle crotch dancing was "distracting" and "out of control." That night I went home and begged my mom to let me quit, just as I had quit Brownies, washing my hair, and 4H. Janet pulled no punches.

"You know who quits? Drips quit. Girls like Bethany up the street who still sucks her thumb quits."

Them there's fightin' words. I didn't mind being called a drip, but being called an elementary school thumb-sucker is where I drew the line. I continued to drag myself in a pouty haze to the church basement, hopelessly convinced that I was getting further and further from my stripping career. I was starting to feel like my calling in life was slipping away from me.

Until one day, Mrs. DeMello pulled out the costume catalog for the recitals.

Hallelujah! My drill sergeant had become my most unlikely guardian angel. Mrs. DeMello's costume catalog was like a treasure trove of inappropriately foxy outfits for tiny girls, including Naughty Little Bo Peep, Sexy Moulin Rouge Girl, and Coy Country Maid. Heaven! You name it, she had it. I found myself eager to sign up for ballet, tap, and modern jazz dancing just to get my paws on more bedazzled clothing. I decided on Naughty Shepherdess, figuring it would fit in with the locals. It was fabulous—hot pink satin, with clip-on curls for my hair, complete with a crook (the rounded cane I would need to tap dance corral my imaginary sheep, obviously). Finally, I had sequins, tassels, and feathers in my life.

Clearly, this was the sign I needed to plan something *big*. I mulled on performing an elaborate burlesque routine for my brother's Cub Scout troop. My mom was the den mother, and I loved getting to accompany them on their group outings. So many boys! My best chance for something exciting would be when we all went to Battleship Cove, the world's largest naval ship museum in Fall River, Massachusetts. The Scouts would have nowhere to run once the show got started—they literally would be my own little captive audience. With my mom in charge I easily squeezed my way into a day of "learning about America." Once we were safely underwater, I could remove my thick winter outerwear and my brother's hand-me-down dungarees and I would give Battleship Cove an exhibit unlike any they'd ever had before. Surely a memorial would be erected in my honor. But oh no—Battleship Cove was not the place for stripping down.

7

On that day, we went through the battleship. No big deal. Lots of gray metal. Whatever. The Cub Scouts and I passed through the main work area, then into the tiny dining hall, and through to the hospital quarantine area, with lots of old military dummies lying on the cots. I sat in a fighter jet, pretended to fire old torpedoes, looked at Japanese motorboats, and admired helicopters. Blah, blah, blah. Torture! I had to suffer through a tour of naval history but was so happy to be with so many of my older brother's friends. I wanted to appear cool and poised. All the boys were excited to go down into the sub, so I happily followed.

We climbed down into the tiny undersea quarters of an old World War II sub tethered to a dock. I have never been so enclosed, so far from air, or so disoriented. However, "nowhere to run" meant we were *all* trapped.

I wish I could have shouted: "Hello boys!! All of this history is making me patriotic! And what is more American than a good old-fashioned strip show?!"

Instead, I had a raging panic attack deep underwater in the submarine. My heart started to race to the point I thought it was going to explode. I was short of breath, and I was fighting back tears as I clutched my mother's arm. That day, I learned that I am claustrophobic. Big time.

I am not proud to report that, stuck in a submarine, I totally lost my shit. I was not a sexy shepherdess—I was more like a deranged mental patient who needs to be ejected from the U-boat if everyone else were to have a chance to survive. Pro tip: get to know your phobias before you disrobe.

My mother had to take me to the dock and sit with me until I calmed down. Any street cred I had with Cub Scout Troop 67 was officially gone. Although you might think my public naval shaming would have been enough to deter me from trying to strip again, like any great unrecognized artist, my setback fueled me forward. I was desperate. People started avoiding me. I would panic and strip for anyone. It was getting ugly. A stripper-vention finally arrived at a desperate hour while I was nude, chasing my babysitter down a large rock at the beach.

"Kevin!! I haven't even busted out my gyrating finale yet—where are you going?? Come back!!!"

I heard my horrified mother, who had caught me in the act, say, "Arden! Arden! Just stop it. You don't see Grandma stripping, do you?"

I didn't really get her logic, but even as a child I knew I did not want to see a nude eighty-year-old Helen Myrin. But part of me really wishes I had—maybe it would have made my stripper obsession seem genetic. I guess Grandma Myrin wasn't touched by the body electric[5] like I was.

You might be wondering what dark hidden feelings my desire to strip was expressing. I've thought a lot about this, and I can honestly say NONE. ZERO. It was probably the most joyful and free I have ever been in my body. All I wanted to be was a Ziegfeld Girl, and I hadn't learned yet that I was supposed to be ashamed of my body. Hell, my adult self wishes I had half of this young lady's freedom and pizzazz getting undressed now as I had then. I'm working on it.

---

5. At the height of my stripping mania, I was also obsessed with the *very* adult movie *Fame*, which I watched all the time on a well-worn Beta copy at the age of seven. Aside from the fun drug use and sexcapades, the climax of the movie is a real tearjerker of a song called "I Sing the Body Electric." Look it up! It is EVERYTHING!!!!!

The Cake Diet

Fuck Atkins! The Keto Diet? To hell with it! Why force yourself to nibble on seeds and rice cakes when you can have your cake and eat it, too? You can be tankini ready by summer if you follow the Cake Diet!

My father, Willy Myrin, had an intricate system for losing weight that involved getting your body so hooked on round, bakery birthday cakes that you actually lost weight when you switched to eating only plain old sheet cakes. The logic behind this system was complex but hinged on the fact that there is less icing per slice on a sheet cake than on a regular round birthday cake. Genius.

Let's just take a beat here and let me explain a few things. The Myrin family has a pretty compulsive genetic makeup. In all honestly, forms of addiction run rampant through the family tree. But not just your standard drinking and smoking compulsions. We can get addicted to anything. I have eaten the same breakfast every day for fifteen years and became so addicted to *Candy Crush* on my phone that within three days of downloading it I developed carpal tunnel and spent $78 on "boosters."

My brother has his own addictions—he's addicted to gadgets, watches, telescopes, you name it. Alarik has purchased so many telescopes that he hasn't used, he should really consider setting up his own observatory. You've got the scopes, bro! Just do it!

But back to my dad and his Cake Diet. Does his system work? You bet! Willy cut an amazing figure. He was a grown man who was shaped like a baby. It was impossible to meet him and not want to shove him into a onesie and carry him around. Being without a child myself, I often contemplated putting my dad in a BabyBjörn and wearing him to my high school reunion.

"What an adorable baby you have! Should infants really be gnawing on sirloin?"

Don't knock being shaped like a baby. It has its advantages. My father was wildly buoyant. Throw him in a body of water and that guy could float like a blowup toy. Exhibit A:

No, that is not a floaty toy. That is a certified public accountant.

Summertime meant body surfing season for Willy Myrin. He could take full naps out at sea. I have never seen anything like it. He could actually cross his feet and put his hands behind his head and nod off in the middle of the ocean like a large, retirement-age sea otter. You better believe that if I had ever been on a boat that capsized with him, I would have let all the other passengers grab the life jackets, because nothing floated better than Willy. I could have surfed on him like a human boogie board and been cozy and warm until we reached safety.

My dad weighed himself every morning to keep tabs on how awesome his numbers were doing. Contrary to all reason, the inventor of the Cake Diet was so obsessed with his weight that when my mom moved his rusty, gigantic hospital scale out into the shed, he actually started running nude across the lawn every morning to compulsively check his weight and detail how his Cake Diet was working. *That* is the kind of commitment you need to be free in your body! Morning, neighbors! Nothing says rise and shine like a baby-shaped accountant with dangly old-man balls traipsing across the lawn to hide in the shed for a few minutes.

"Nothing to see here! Keep it moving, people!"

If you don't weigh yourself round the clock, how will you truly know if that third helping of the Fourth of July "God Bless America!" sheet cake was the thing that finally made you lose those pesky five pounds?

You were always taking your life into your hands when you went into the Myrin family fridge. My dad had a two-decade-long habit of making bologna sandwiches and "aging" them on top of the fridge for a day or two. This aging process produces a result that is similar to toasting a sandwich, but instead of your lunch being crusty from coming straight out of the toaster, it is crusty with age and mold. That toasty, crusty sandwich was not bought at a Quiznos—it was made in 1992.

Willy also had an old food collection, much like a foodie aficionado might have different vintages of wine or cheese in the home. Some chocolate Santas had been in our house since 1983. "This is a great vintage in Russell Stover's St. Nicks—1994 was a wonderful year. The chocolate had a hint of caramel in it." Don't be afraid to collect food. It is way cheaper than collecting Fabergé eggs and a lot less douchey!

There are many Willy Myrin–tested ways to lose weight, and he was incredibly loyal to each method. He basically ate one food item for breakfast, lunch, and dinner for months on end. Then, without rhyme or reason, he would jump ship and move on to the next homemade diet that struck his fancy. Food products he tested eating exclusively for months on end included Nibs; Oreos (regular, Double Stuf, and Golden Double Stuf); industrial-size, teddy bear–shaped containers of Teddy Grahams; hard pretzels; fat-free American cheese slices (you don't want it to be bad for you); fat-free bologna (see fat-free American cheese slices); mugs of Lipton tea prepared with skim milk and fourteen Splenda packets (see two previous entries); mint M&M's; black-and-white cookies; and Oysterettes crackers dipped in the three main food groups—shrimp cocktail sauce, peanut butter, and Cheez Whiz (you know, for protein).

If none of the food offerings are your cup of tea, do not despair. Calories don't count when you eat standing up. Because of this—and the fact that my brother and I are disgusting dining companions—my father refused to eat with the family. Instead, Big Willy hovered around the table like a hungry seagull, and you never knew when his greedy little hands were going to dive bomb and steal the food off your plate. According to Willy, the calories in other people's food also do not count, and taste better.

To this day I eat defensively—I finish a meal in thirty seconds or less. This comes from years of guarding my food from the Red Baron hovering over my shoulder, waiting to attack and scoop up my mashed potatoes with his thumb and dirty pointer finger. (Oh yes, his hands were dirty. Recently, my brother and I realized that our father never washed his hands.) Yum yum! Also, you are much more likely to get away with stealing someone's food if you are already standing.

I recommend test-driving the eating-off-other-people's-plates technique with your own family before you invite friends over for a dinner party. Odd as it may seem, some people don't like it when you put your dirty fingers in their spaghetti. Go figure! My friend Sheryle once almost stabbed Willy's hand with a fork when he made a move for her piece of angel food cake.

If you *must* entertain friends, make sure that your guests are comfortable by making your home and dining area as inviting as possible. According to Willy, nothing sets the scene and impresses your friends at a dinner party like a television blaring tabloid entertainment news programs like *The Insider*, *TMZ*, or *Extra* two feet from your dining table.

The Myrins even upped the ante and tested out four different televisions playing four different channels from four different rooms during mealtime. Ooh-la-la! How European! Who wants to make boring chitchat about the arts or current events when you can make fun of Mario Lopez in the kitchen and guess the secret celebrity having a birthday on *Entertainment Tonight* in the dining room? "Happy birthday to Katherine Heigl, who today turns twenty-nine . . . again!"

A few summers ago, my mother decided to throw a barbecue for our neighbors. With the threat of having to dine without

Harvey Levin talking at us and us having to actually make conversation with other humans al fresco, Big Willy saved the day with a special battery-powered TV he bought just for the occasion. Thank GOD! I can't imagine what I would have talked about with anyone if there hadn't been a news story about Gigi Hadid's latest bikini wax blaring from the new TV on the lawn.

Another one of Willy's weight loss theories was: "A movie a day keeps the belly away."

Yes, Willy went to a matinee every single day. Oh, he loved the flicks, but mostly he discovered that if you go to the movies, that's two hours when you won't be near a kitchen. Additionally, you will be the envy of all your friends because you will have seen *everything*—and I mean EVERYTHING! Because of his commitment to looking fly in his pants, my dad saw all the *Twilight* movies (he was Team Jacob, FYI: "Boy, that shape-shifter has a nice torso!"). Guess who was at opening day of *Spice World*? Yep, your favorite man baby. *Hannah Montana: The Movie* too low brow for my father? I think not.

"Hey—I think she's hot!"

"She's a child," I responded.

"So? She's still hot!"

Touché, my friend, touché. You name it, he saw it.

But the most extreme form of dieting happened over the holidays one year. I found an old hammer left out on my parents' kitchen counter. It immediately struck me as odd, because no one in my family is handy at all. I come from a proud line of draft dodgers and gentleman farmers. Since I had no memory of the handyman coming by, I put the hammer back in the tool kit and went on with my day. Hours later I heard Willy screaming, "Who moved my cookie hammer?! Goddammit—WHERE IS MY COOKIE HAMMER??!" It slowly dawned on me that the cookie hammer he was referring to was the gigantic, rusty hammer I had put away earlier.

I had heard of the Cookie Diet but was mind boggled at what the hammer could be used for. Apparently, building on the success of his experiments with aging sandwiches, Willy had thrown desserts into the mix. He was buying snickerdoodles the size of dinner plates from the local ice cream parlor and "aging" them until they were rock hard. His theory was that you can't eat cookies as fast if there is no way to actually bite into them!

Enter the Cookie Hammer. You just smash the cookie with a hammer to break off a piece, and enjoy said piece by dunking it into hot tea (with fourteen packets of Splenda in it) and sucking it down. Why hadn't anyone thought of this sooner? It's only a matter of time before Big Willy Myrin's Cake Diet and Cookie Hammer sweep Hollywood! If you see Mrs. Hailey Bieber with a cookie in her hand and hammer in her purse, just know that she has caught the fever!

This leads me to the fashionistas among my readers. If you absolutely need to have accessories as a fun part of your makeover, and carrying a hammer isn't your thing, fret not! Willy Myrin owned and carried around a personal soda cooler since 1978. The *same* cooler. It was sort of a fun man purse/refrigerator for the gentleman on the go. It held six sodas and a spot for a round ice pack. My mother sewed numerous carrying covers for it over the years, to keep it fresh and jaunty. For those of you making your own cooler cover at home, she found that denim is the sportiest and sturdiest of all the covers. Think of it as a fun Bermuda bag for sodas. You can make covers to go with all your outfits!

My father brought his trusty purse-cooler to weddings, bars, restaurants, funerals, you name it! My mother tried to talk him out of bringing it to *my wedding*, as in: "I'm sure the caterer will serve Diet Coke, since Arden paid for the Diet Coke bar for you." Nope! My wedding was not serving *his* Diet Coke! Every man for himself! You don't want to owe anyone anything. Ever.

At my wedding, Willy also shoved a can of Diet Coke into each of his jacket pockets and carried a portable bendy straw to consume his drinks. Willy was quite a clotheshorse and paid top dollar for a finely tailored jacket or suit. All the Myrins are the proud inheritors of a very specific build—we have the longest torsos and shortest inseams in all the land. To this day, I do not fit in a one-piece bathing suit. I am five feet four inches tall, of which five feet two inches is my torso. We are like a pack of human Corgi dogs. Just picture a Corgi in a custom-made cashmere sport coat with a six-pack of TaB shoved into each pocket. I bet designers were delighted to see their latest fashions stretched to the ground with twenty-four ounces of soda shoved into each pocket like liquid saddlebags. I smell a fashion trend!!! Watch out, Marc Jacobs!

Willy's soda man purse.

Being an avid convertible driver caused some problems for Willy, as he always drove with a fresh can of Caffeine-Free Diet Coke with a bendy straw in it. The second he hit the open road with the top down, soda in hand, the straw went flying out of the can and usually landed in his lap, leaving a gigantic brown wet stain on his crotch. So it's actually a stroke of genius that he arrived at social events with his own refreshments, as a host may find a man with a big wet crotch stain not to be the ultimate dining companion.

When the cooler was on its last legs in 2006, Willy refused to replace it. Instead, he hired Walter, a Little Compton architect and boat builder, to rebuild the cooler from the inside out. Walter was the perfect expert to perform major surgery on Willy's true love, because the cooler was composed of fiberglass and the boat-builder side of Walter was used to working with that material. I wonder if when he graduated from architecture school Walter imagined he would be working on such an illustrious commission as building a home for cans of TaB.

My father was happily married to his soda man purse for thirty-nine years. His union with his soda cooler was the only committed relationship he did not enter into on a dare.

XO, JJ

I truly believe it just takes one. One human who sees your magic and loves you to help survive a tricky childhood full of mixed signals—love and taunting, laughter and cruelty. It can be a parent, a teacher, a sibling, a friend. Clearly, I did not win the dad lottery. Willy was who he was. He was not interested in being a father. He was not really interested in people in general. Mostly he liked to nap, watch *MASH* reruns, and, as you just learned, eat cake. It didn't help that he was a very active alcoholic until his liver crashed—the same day the stock market crashed in 1987—at which point he was sent to a thirty-day treatment program.

Miraculously, he never drank again (to the best of my knowledge), which was a huge gift. However, his personality stayed the same. He didn't go into AA or join a sober community—the main difference when he returned from rehab was that he filled our bar with candy instead of alcohol.

Thankfully, he was not the only adult in the house. I am so grateful that I got the best mom in the world (with all due respect to all the moms out there). Janet was funny, loving, supportive, and hilarious. She thought being a mom was the most fun thing in the whole wide world and set about giving me and my brother Alarik room to play and make things and soar.

Janet wanted four kids. Willy wanted zero. So they compromised and had two. I think my parents had an agreement that me and my brother were *Janet's* kids—almost like a divorced couple with the mom getting sole custody. Except they were married, and Willy lived in our house. I know this because Willy used to say, "I told your mom if she wanted kids, she'd have to be the one to deal with you." Or the advice he gave me and my brother—"Never have kids! They will take all of your money."

I think Janet was perfectly happy with the arrangement. My brother, my mom, and I were the Three Musketeers. The three of us would do everything together—play games, go to amusement parks, even go on family trips. Willy used to say that the three of us going on a holiday was his vacation from the family. It never really bothered me that he didn't come with us. I was so used to him not being a part of our lives that we all just sort of adapted, and during the '80s dads in general seemed to get a bit of a pass from being too involved in child-rearing.

Calm, unflappable, pragmatic, and funny, Mama Bear Janet Myrin was a roll-with-the-punches kind of gal. She was an early bird, organized, list-making Virgo who nevertheless embraced and accepted the fact that she had given birth to two messy, late-night oddballs. Genetics run deep, and my dad's nocturnal bloodline dictated the circadian rhythms of me and my brother.

I have been an insomniac my entire life. It's not that I can't sleep so much as I have absolutely no desire to sleep while it's dark out. Nighttime is the right time! My brother and my father and I were all wired like vampires and have been that way since we were born. No matter how exhausted I am during the day, as the sun goes down my inner Edward Cullen wakes up. I don't hit my stride until midnight or one in the morning, which is when my charms are in full effect.

The fact that Janet had given birth to two vampires became clear very early on. When Alarik and I were infants, my mom would put us in our cribs at night, and the later it got the more wide awake we became. We would stand in our little cribs, grasping the bars, waiting for someone to come play with us. As babies, we were fairly out of it all day, but then, as the moon rose, we sprang to life, cooing, giggling, and laughing. Like two little raccoons, we would blossom into full-blown creatures of the night before her eyes.

Janet attempted to be a dutiful mother and would try to stay up with us until we fell asleep. It was a fruitless effort. Without fail, she would eventually pass out, and we would just stay up entertaining ourselves for hours, ready to party. Every night when the clock struck midnight, for the first time during the day, Janet's tiny brood didn't seem like they were totally drugged out. Eventually she just waved the white flag to our circadian rhythms, allowing us to stay up, playing, dreaming, and crafting.

Janet and her little night owl.

As long as we were making things, our sleep patterns were A-OK with her. My mom wanted us to get to know our imaginations so we could be happy and soar in the world. Her number-one rule for me and Alarik was "Don't be a drip."

Being a drip was the worst offense under Janet's roof. There is no flair, no pizzazz to being a drip.

Being a drip includes being a tattletale, being too clingy, being a poor sport, being a crybaby, being a wuss, being a mama's boy, being too anal, being unable to entertain yourself, being too needy, having no imagination, or just being an all-around dud.

People of all ages are able to commit the crime of being a drip. Once a year, when my mom was required to help out in my classroom (none of this "moms should always be in the classroom" hullabaloo that goes on today), she would come home with very honest reviews of my classmates. "That kid Monica? She's a drip."

To be fair, Monica *was* a drip. She'd greet you with a dead fish handshake and spend the entire gym class sitting in the corner eating her grape-flavored Lip Smacker lip balm. We Myrins may have eaten cookies with a hammer, but at least we didn't eat lip balm.

"Those sisters, Debbie and Denise? *Both* drips—and their mother's a drip, too." Their offense? Not being twins, but dressing in *identical* outfits every day until puberty.

"What's wrong with their mother? They're *twelve*, not six. Why does she always dress them like they're about to be on a Christmas card?"

You have to admit, Janet did have a point. It was weird that two growing girls would both wear red plaid jumpers, red plaid hair ribbons, and navy knee socks on Tuesdays, then matching kitten sweatshirts, pigtails, and overalls on Thursdays. Janet was like a stealth bomber with her judgments. She would just sweep in under the radar and—*boom*—bomb delivered on target.

"That girl Shelley? There's something creepy about her. She looks like she chews on her hair, and she's in middle school."

Was my mom a little harsh? Maybe. Was she correct? Absolutely. Shelley wasn't a drip, but she *was* creepy. How did Janet nail it so fast? How could she put her finger exactly on the creepy button? I hadn't even told my mom that every time I got invited over to Shelley's house she would tie me up with rope or chase me through the woods with a bow and arrow. Maybe that was Shelley's early way of flirting.

Janet was equally hard on the boys.

"That kid Erik? He's a freak. He barks at the vacuum cleaner, and his dad sells meat rabbits from their yard. Something's wrong with that kid."

Well, that one was pretty obvious to the naked eye, but she was so succinct in her critique.

Alarik and I were not spared. When we would go out in public, occasionally our blood sugar would drop and one of us would end up on the floor clinging to her wide whale corduroy trousers in the aisle of the general store.

"You're really being a nudge right now. Stop hanging on my pants leg. I didn't set out to raise drag kids."

While not as bad as being a drip, being a nudge or a drag are both gateway drugs to the same destination. They included whining, begging for candy, being a brat, saying that you were bored, having your feelings hurt too easily, or overall not being funny.

Janet believed in me and my brother as independent creatures at a very young age. I graduated from high school at seventeen, not because I was smart but because Janet decided when I was four that it was time to send me to school. She was done. The school tried to reject me, claiming I was a year too young to attend, but Janet didn't care and showed up with me for kindergarten anyway.

Once enrolled, she had no patience for bullshit school requests.

"Didn't you go to the planetarium last year? That place is lame. Who wants to stare at a ceiling for two hours? Waste of time. They just don't have the budget for anything interesting. You can play hooky today if you want, and make things."

Moms, don't fear hooky day—it will make you the most popular mom on earth!

Janet gave us one free hooky day a year. We never knew when it was coming, and she would pull me and my brother from school, declaring: "Hooky Day!" She would whisk us down to climb on the rocks by the beach, have a picnic, and then drive over to all the fancy large summer houses that sat empty nine months a year. We would go hang out on the wide porches of the empty seaside homes of rich people and watch the waves crash, and then we would peer in the windows to see who had what kind of furnishings.

"Huh! You'd think that the Kellers would spring for a fancier ottoman."

Our school also participated in the annual Oxfam Fast to raise money for starving kids in Africa. The way it worked was we would all fast for the day to see what it felt like to be hungry, and we would donate the money that we would have spent on lunch to the kids in Africa.

"That is so stupid. Of course they can have some money, but why should you kids go hungry, too? My kids will just be drips with low blood sugar. Homey don't play that game." (*In Living Color* was a big hit in the Myrin household.)

On Oxfam Fast Day, Janet donated money to Oxfam, but in protest sent me and my brother with the biggest lunches anyone had ever seen. We each got a gigantic bucket of Kentucky Fried Chicken for lunch that day, complete with mashed potatoes and biscuits.

"Share the bucket with the other kids whose parents are too chickenshit to feed them today."

Needless to say, my mom was popular with the other kids, too. She was the den mother for my brother's Cub Scout troop. Each week she would shoot from the hip about what she was going to teach.

"Okay, boys. Today I am going to teach you how to put on a Broadway musical!"

She had never produced a Broadway musical, or even been in a play, but she loved Broadway and wanted kids to know about what was possible out in the world. So she taught the six-year-old sons of farmers, lobstermen, and plumbers how to produce the next *Hello, Dolly!* She even constructed her own flip book to illustrate her point.

"First, you need a story. Without a story, there is no show to put on. You see these people here, boys? Those are the actors. You need the actors to tell the story. This lady over here is the director. The director is the person who tells the actors what to do. Then you need a producer. Do you know who the producer is, boys?"

Silence. They stared at a drawing of a fat man smoking a cigar.

"The producer is the most important person on the show because he is the MONEY MAN. And without the money man, none of this is possible."

I recently ran into one of the guys who was in her Cub Scout troop, and he told me that to this day, every time he goes to see a movie, he waits for the credits to see who the producer is because that's the money man, the most important person on the show. I want to be the money lady someday, but that is a whole other story.

One day, Janet couldn't make it to the troop meeting, and Willy had to take over. His plan for the day was much different—he decided to teach the boys of Little Compton how to make a craft. Like my mom, he also had never executed what he was about to teach the boys.

"Okay, kids, today we are going to make extension cords."

What!? My dad was not handy, he was not an electrician, and he was most likely slightly buzzed. Nevertheless, he had some wires, some plugs to attach to them, and a will to teach seven-year-old boys about electricity.

"First, you cut the length of the cord you need. Then you attach this thing here—you just jam it on. Goddammit! Well, you get the idea. Hold this, kid. I'm gonna just go for it."

And then he plugged in his Frankenstein electrical contraption. "Argh!!!! Jesus Christ!!"

He had blown out the socket. He's lucky he didn't electrocute himself and start a fire that day. It's probably for the best that he was not the main adult in charge of me and my brother.

For the most part, Willy was pretty hands-off with our day-to-day parenting growing up. He taught us not to smoke by letting us take puffs from his ever-present Lark cigarette, and not to drink by letting us take sips of his Gordon's Gin. As long as you followed his number-one rule—don't wake Willy Myrin before noon—you were pretty much in the clear with what you could get away with. But there were a few things that he had to take the bullet for. Although generally unflappable, Janet just did not have the temperament to teach the two of us how to drive. You see, Alarik lacks peripheral vision, and I lack mental focus.

Janet had a healthier fear of death than Willy Myrin did. Willy had no regard for his own personal safety, which made him a natural fit to take on the life-threatening role of Myrin family driving instructor. Willy was on duty whether he liked it or not.

Little Compton is great for driving if you never plan to merge lanes or go over thirty-five miles per hour. Willy had higher hopes for his kids and decided to start me with the advanced driving course. No puttering around on back roads for me!

Willy brought me to the fastest highway in the area, and possibly in the United States: Route 128 outside of Boston. Route 128 is not for the faint of heart—it is five lanes full of aggressive Massholes driving bumper to bumper. Route 128 is a lot like the Autobahn, if the Autobahn were filled with people sporting 1980s mall bangs and mullets tailgating you in uninsured Camaros. Even the grandmas will pass you in the breakdown lane and shout: "Pussy!"

Willy drove me up there and parked in the parking lot of a Roy Rogers. He got out of the driver's side of his car and took his man purse/cooler to the passenger side. He tossed me the keys, busted out a TaB, and taught me how to drive.

"All right. Here's all you need to know. He who hesitates gets killed."

"Huh?"

Silence.

Willy was already distracted, searching through his pockets for stray Teddy Grahams. I was nervous.

"What about allowing three car lengths, or staying at least one hundred feet behind an emergency vehicle?"

I had not spent all summer taking Driver's Ed in a mini mall next to a water park to not debate the finer points of vehicular management.

"He who hesitates gets killed; that's it," he repeated, as if I had not heard him the first time. "What are you waiting or? GO!!"

And that was it. That was all the fatherly advice I was going to get. And it turns out that it was all I needed. It works in every situation. I adjusted the seat and checked my rearview mirrors. Willy turned on his oldies station and I floored it.

My mom was very tightlipped about the whole thing when I got home.

"All good? You know how to drive now?"

That was the only parenting Janet was willing to hand over to my father. The rest of me and my brother was totally created by her.

As I got older my mom had new rules. She wasn't the most introspective lady, and whenever life got emotionally complicated, she would come up with things to cheer us up. Each time a heart got broken, a beloved grandparent passed away, or a job ended, Janet would put on her thinking cap and figure out how to make you feel better.

She would suggest a trip to TJ Maxx to find a cute cashmere cape, or a pom-pom lamp, or a Pucci knockoff caftan for the beach. She liked things to be upbeat *no matter what*. She didn't indulge you if you were feeling sorry for yourself. She would give you a hug and allow you to have a day or two of moping, and then she would intervene. There was one time I was feeling particularly low after a show I wrote and filmed a pilot for was not picked up. I had been wallowing around my apartment in my sweatpants for at least forty-eight hours when the phone rang.

"You need to watch the Katy Perry documentary."

"I'm sorry, what?"

"YOU need to get up from the couch, dust yourself off, and watch the Katy Perry documentary."

You couldn't say no to Janet. So I watched it. And you know what? She was right. She was right about most things. Watching Katy sobbing in a tunnel before getting rocketed up to the stage to perform in Brazil moments after receiving a text from Russell Brand that he wanted a divorce was inspirational. If Katy Perry could put on a bra that shot whipped cream *and* pull herself up by the bootstraps, so could I. The show must go on.

The fact that my mom recommended Katy Perry to me was not as unusual as it sounds. She found a lot of joy and solace in pop culture. Janet would text me things out of the blue, like: "Justin Bieber is liquid gold," or "I can draw Sarah Jessica Parker's face, but I can't draw Lady Gaga's face." I'm not sure who was requesting celebrity portraits from her.

One day, the oddest thing happened. At the age of seventy-five, my mom gave herself a nickname. I didn't know that you could give yourself a nickname, and I didn't know you could do it in your mid-seventies, but I loved her flair. I know this because she started signing all her texts and e-mails "XO, JJ." *JJ? Who is JJ?* One of her e-mails included: "You know everyone thinks Britney Spears is very social but she's actually a very private person. XO, JJ." Bold call. Like JJ Abrams or JJ Walker. DY-NO-MITE! YASSSS JJ!

✳ ·
· ✳
✳

Straight Outta Little Compton

Are you tired of stoplights and people and chiefs of police
who can read? Are you ready to party like it's 1699? Then
perhaps Little Compton, Rhode Island, is just the place
for you to raise your own brood. My parents left New York
City—population 8,244,910—to move to Little Compton,
Rhode Island. Human population: 3,512. Cow population:
278. This is the place where my parents figured my brother
and I could learn how to make our own fun.

Growing up in my particular family wasn't the only thing
that gave me an unusual perspective to navigate the world. I
also happened to have been raised in what felt like the smallest
town in America. On the one hand, Little Compton, Rhode
Island, is heaven. It is the most magical tiny seaside New
England setting. The few people who have stumbled upon it
return year after year to bask in the joyful otherworldliness of
the beach village—fireflies, fruit stands, bike rides, and salt
air aplenty.

But if you dream of a life with bright lights and the big
city, growing up in my hometown is not exactly going to give
you the toolbox you need to take the world of Hollywood by
storm. Even if you grew up in the most sheltered backwoods
town and you dream of a life of glamour—take heart.
Everyone needs a place to run away from, and this was it for
me. (If only our general store had had a theater attached to it,

I might not have ever left, as Little Compton, Rhode Island, remains my happy place to this day.)

All aboard the chicken caboose!

Little Compton, est. 1682, used to have three restaurants, but two of them burned to the ground. Currently, it has zero stoplights, zero high schools, one local doctor who took a shit in the third hole at the local golf course, one train car that is parked in a field and is inhabited by two hundred chickens, one cell phone provider (we just got our first cell tower at the town dump), and one toothless elderly lady who smokes a corncob pipe and hangs out at the cash register of the general store (and at home answers the door nude for the local delivery boys). So we are no Podunk town!

There are also hobbies aplenty! Whether your interests include tractor pulls, drag racing, or drinking, Little Compton has something for everyone. My mother's friend Clare keeps herself busy with the pet yaks she raises in her backyard, giving us regular "yak reports."

"Little Elvis only wants to be fed by baby bottles."

Little Compton has the feel of living on an island, as it is an isolated peninsula surrounded by sandy shores, rocky beaches, and jagged, wind-blown cliffs over the sea. The main village looks like time stopped about four hundred years ago. There is the sense that you could actually meet both a Pilgrim and a Native American chief for a powwow over coffee if you wanted to.

The town center is called the Commons, where the main commerce occurs. The nerve center of the Commons is Wilbur's, Little Compton's only store. Wilbur's is an old school general store. It has penny candy, paint, a butcher, "store cheese," hammers, cast iron pans, sawdust, rat poison, chains for your tires, goat food, fishing boots, and a beauty department consisting of rubbing alcohol and AIM toothpaste. Think of it as our town's Nordstrom.

The town Commons (aka the Times Square of Little Compton, consisting of Wilbur's General Store and a diner).

Not only does Little Compton have no stoplights, it also has no four-way intersections. When it was founded, the only place you could put a bar was at a four-way intersection, so the

Puritans made sure that all the roads met in a way that was not quite direct. I am proud to say the roads (and inhabitants) of Little Compton remain slightly off to this day.

In the summertime, Lil' Compton gets a lil' fancier. There are some Lexuses added to the lineup of pickup trucks at Wilbur's—but this is no Hamptons crowd, as there is nothing to buy, do, or eat in town. The best part of the "summer people" are the nicknames they have, ladies with monikers like Buffy, Go-Go, Kitty, Peanuts, Pookah, and Polly, and even a man named Carol (who is married to a woman named Bobby). My favorite is a lovely woman named Pussy Hammer. When I waitressed at the golf club and tended to Pussy and her friends, I would dissolve into fits of giggles whenever she signed her name.

"I think I will have the clams. What do you want, Pussy?"

At least Pussy Hammer wasn't hanging out with the golf champ Dick Wood. That would have been too much for me to handle.

Part of the fun of the town is the sense that no one is really in charge. We have no mayor, just the head of the town council. So the live-and-let-live attitude was the perfect place for my family to go about doing our own thang—eating cookies with a hammer and napping. For much of my youth we had a chief of police named Terry who I am told was illiterate (but you know how small towns are; that could have just been a rumor. If it was true, it really didn't matter because we all LOVED him.) but who we kept voting back into office because he was a fun guy. Sure, he might not have been able read, but as no real crime happened in Little Compton anyway, being affable seemed to be the main trait needed to enforce the law in our little town. After an election, Terry would drive around and give everyone in town a big thumbs-up for voting him back in.

Rhode Island is a funny little state—during my childhood it was the mafia capital of the country. Our state capital, Providence, had arguably the best mayor ever, Buddy Cianci. In the 1980s, Buddy was the mayor who got arrested during his tenure for having an off-duty police officer drive him over to his wife's lover's house so he could beat him up with a lit cigarette, an ashtray, and a fireplace log, and then put the cigarette out on his penis. Holler!

Buddy got arrested, thrown in jail, served his time, and then got out and was reelected. He wore a full toupee he nicknamed The Squirrel, had his own pasta sauce called Mayor's Choice, and his own Mayor's Choice Coffee. While Buddy was mayor the second time, he got caught in a financial scandal and was thrown in jail again. When he got released, he would have probably been reelected a third time had he decided to run, but instead he went on to become one of the most popular DJs in the state.

What I'm trying to say is: Rhode Island has a pretty big laissez-faire attitude. It is not as insane as the "Live Free or Die" people up in New Hampshire (I always get the feeling they will kill you if you try to rein them in). But more on that later.

Growing up we did not own a key to our house, and my parents would frequently leave their cars unlocked with the keys in the ignition. That stopped when someone broke into our garage and riffled through my mom's car. They didn't take anything. I guess the burglar wasn't looking for scratched CDs of the original Broadway cast recording of *Starlight Express*.

One winter when I was seven, the town was abuzz. We had a real live burglar who was caught robbing one of the unlocked summer homes. Who knew there was a demand for old mothballs and glass lamps with nautical ropes? Our very own criminal—this was big time! And a little bit tricky. Tricky because Little Compton had no jail, much less a police station. Our police were stationed in a room in the basement of the town hall, which was right next to the building that housed the International Odd Fellows Society,[6] which meant we had no holding space for our little thief.

Ever resourceful, Terry the chief of police came up with a plan. Rumor has it he got out some rope and tied the burglar to a chair and called on all the local farmers to come down and guard the perp with their rakes and hoes. Can you imagine a more emasculating punishment?

"If you try to escape, I will rake the shit out of your balls!"

For many years the biggest unsolved crime we had was when the mail in Little Compton seemed to go missing. No one could figure out who the mail thief was. Eventually, Team Police Force One cracked the case! The culprit? Poe the Crow, an actual crow a local woman kept for a pet. Poe had figured out how to open mailboxes with his beak and was flying around the neighborhood stealing all the mail out of the mailboxes. Because stealing mail is a federal crime, Poe was put under house arrest and remained an "indoor crow" for the rest of his days.

Everything radically changed in the late eighties when a local police officer discovered that Little Compton was one of

---

6. Quite honestly, growing up I never quite knew what or who the International Odd Fellows Society (aka the IOOF) was. Judging by the title, I felt that my dad would fit right in! Doing a little googling, I found that it appears to be a fraternal organization on par with the Lions Club.

three ports used in a huge international drug trafficking scheme. Our sleepy little harbor was so small, no one would ever think that giant bricks of hash were being smuggled in, rolled up in "imported rugs" from South Africa. That drug bust was the third largest in the nation at the time, and the town benefited from receiving a percentage of the bust—our police unit received a windfall of a few million dollars.

All of a sudden our police force was equipping itself with night-vision goggles, high-tech shooting ranges, and a pimped-out *Miami Vice*-style police speed boat. It was bizarre to be in an old rowboat and see Terry blowing past standing on the front of a yacht that could double as the set for Jay-Z's "Big Pimpin'" video.

The downside to this bounty is that the police are now armed and looking for action. Who wants to have fun toys if you can't use them? Equipped with gadgets you would find in a *Mission Impossible* movie, Little Compton's finest are now just waiting for *anything* to bust. I pity the teen who wants to commit a prank in our town. Our police force has so much high-tech equipment, they could scan your retinas should you dare lie about shoplifting a Charleston Chew from Wilbur's.

Little Compton's finest are not fucking around. If teenagers get caught smashing mailboxes with a bat today (a popular Little Compton teen pastime), they would not have the luxury of being tied to a chair and taunted by farmers. No, they would be held in the most elaborate jail center a small town has ever seen, complete with an indoor firing range and a high-speed emergency patrol vehicle that is actually a fire truck painted blue.

Just because our police are like Robocops does not mean that the criminals have gotten more sophisticated. Our local newspaper always lists the most amazing crime reports: "Local cow tipped over, tractor suspected in the tip." Here's a gem my mother once sent me from the "Crime Report":

> Police were called to Anthony House senior housing
> on Middle Road at 7:51 p.m. after two neighbors had
> a dispute over the pronunciation of the word "Italian."
> One told the other that he is Italian and does not
> appreciate the word being pronounced "Eye-talian."
> They were advised to stay away from each other.

Tractor pulls were a big hit on the weekends when I was a kid, as was the local annual Chicken Barbecue, complete with a bounce house, carnies, and the big town excitement—the pole greasing contest. No, it was not a strange sex show starring Pilgrims. It involved a real live telephone pole that Terry would cover in Crisco and bacon grease, and people would try to shimmy up to the top like rhesus monkeys. The big prize was a twenty-dollar bill waiting for you at the summit! I wanted that twenty so bad.

Unfortunately, I have no upper body strength and never made it even five feet off the ground. The same kid won it every year—creepy Jeffrey, who spent too much time climbing the ropes in gym class. He claimed it was "practice for the pole-greasing contest," but I'm pretty sure he just liked the feeling of the rope rubbing his own pole.

One of the most exciting holidays in Little Compton is the Fourth of July. Not because of any official celebrations—we lost our privileges with those years ago. As a child, it was always very exciting to go to the town Commons for the bonfire and fireworks display. The purpose of the bonfire was to raise money to help maintain the local Village Improvement Society's building—the Brownell House—located in the town Commons.

The bonfire was exciting because it was extremely dangerous. As with our town politics, no one seemed to be in charge of the bonfire. Basically for the whole month of June, the townspeople would just throw unwanted wooden items in a gigantic pile near the baseball field, which happened to be located directly next to the Brownell House. People would pile anything flammable—old desks and chairs, tables and brooms, rowboats, lobster traps, you name it! If it was flammable, it got thrown on the pile. There never seemed to be any rhyme or reason as to the construction of the huge wooden beast—the more the merrier. Then on the Fourth of July, we would set it ablaze and watch the burning fun!

Without fail, the flames would get a little out of control and start to blow toward the pretty old Brownell House. Basically, year after year, the fundraising bonfire would almost burn down the house that the Village Improvement Society was trying to raise money for. The flames would lap at and singe the roof of the old beauty, making everybody nervous, but excited, too. The local police rescue vehicle (aka our blue fire truck) would be on hand to douse out the flames if they got too crazy.

Eventually the good ladies of the society put their foot down, and the bonfire was deemed unsafe. But people like fire. And where there is a will there is a way. My mother's office partner Adolf[7] puts on one of the greatest illegal fireworks displays this side of the Mississippi. Watch out, Macy's Fourth of July celebration!

---

7. Despite the historical connotation of the name, I assure you *this* Adolf is the best guy in the whole wide world. Really, I've seen him cry at a funeral.

Adolf makes numerous treks up to New Hampshire, where they really take the "Live Free or Die" motto to heart. These reckless and rebellious citizens aren't going to have The Man tell them who can and can't set off homemade pyrotechnic shows. They are going to live free or they are going to DIE, Motherfuckers!!!!

Adolf drives the five hours up north and piles as many fireworks into his vehicle as humanly possible, illegally smuggling them over many borders back to Rhode Island. He does this trip numerous times throughout the winter, stocking up on cherry bombs and roman candles, bottle rockets and jumping jacks. Adolf never has his party on the same date in July, as it is illegal, and our cops—always looking for action— might show up in tanks and wearing infrared goggles. The invitation to Adolf's festivities happens when you receive a very last-minute phone call sometime between July 2 and July 6 telling you to show up at his house in the middle of the woods at sunset. Upon arrival, you see all the fireworks lined up, nailed to wooden boards in the middle of his field. Young and old alike arrive to see Adolf's display.

There is the usual chitchat for an hour or so before it is sufficiently dark. Adolf fills an old army jeep full of ice and beer. Mostly you wait for the sun to go down standing around an old jeep, getting drunk, and in years past, avoiding Adolf's dogs. Adolf owned two wiener dogs, Rusty and Ruby. Rusty and Ruby *hated* men. This was clear because they liked to attack men's balls—big time. Rusty could jump many feet off the ground from a seated position and could even nip at the sack of a pro basketball player. Adolf put Rusty on self-imposed house arrest for lunging at the mailman's balls a few years back. (Perhaps he and Poe the Crow could form a support group.)

When Adolf's fireworks display begins, it is incredible. Adolf and his son lay on their bellies and crawl across the field lighting all the fireworks at once—the entire show is one big finale. The most exciting part is that although most of them rocket up into the sky as they are supposed to, a good many of Adolf's fireworks rocket toward the crowd, the roof of his house, or (one time) his mother-in-law, who sat in a lawn chair for a front-row view of the action. People bring their babies and toddlers and let them run free. Most of them run right toward the incoming missiles, and no one seems to bat an eye.

The crazier and more haphazard the rockets become, the closer the crowd inches toward the lighting of them. No one seems worried that either Adolf or his son are going to blow up themselves and everyone else with them as they put on this wild extravaganza. I think most people want to see how close they can get to actually being lit on fire. The entire evening ends with a BANG from the end of a tiny homemade cannon that one of the neighbors built.

Fourth of July is not the only holiday honored by the good people of

One tiny cannon coming right up!

Little Compton. We may be small, but we love a parade! The Memorial Day parade is a high point of the year. The action consists of people marching twice around the town Commons. As Little Compton also doesn't have a high school, we borrow students from neighboring high schools and ship them in to act as our own marching band!

Dressed head to toe in New England wool majorette outfits, these teens descend on our town and razzle-dazzle us with their Phillip Souza marching songs and baton moves. The highlight each year is taking bets on who will be the first majorette to fall, as the heat coupled with double-boiled wool invariably causes heat stroke. Girls start fainting like flies during the lengthy speeches in the Commons. One by one these eager teens crumple to the ground, only to be left in a pile of royal blue and mustard yellow wool and hair scrunchies.

Veterans of all ages dress in their regalia to march in the

My hat was catnip to bees and drunk teenagers!

parade. One year it rained, but the show must go on! The parade took place with people marching twice around the inside of the school gym. The local butcher had been in the Korean War and was dressed in his uniform, complete with his old rifle. He forgot it was loaded, and it accidentally went off inside the gymnasium.

Another elderly man's pistol accidently fired at his own foot when he was using the urinal. (People were advised to check their firearms for ammunition after that year.)

I had my own disaster at a parade. Our town was celebrating its tricentennial one year when I was a child. One of JJ's specialties (if you are enough of a wildcard to give yourself a nickname at the age of seventy-five, you better believe I am going to honor it!) was making a jaunty headpiece for any occasion. She never met an Easter bonnet she could not replicate. That year she really took her millenary skills up a notch: she baked the town a birthday cake and stuck it on my head. It was fabulous. It was a skimmer hat like you might see on a man in a barbershop quartet, but it was totally made out of cake! The cake was fastened to my skull with red, white, and blue ribbons and bobby pins. The cake hat was covered in white icing, complete with icing flowers and birthday candles coming off my head. I was the belle of the Tricentennial Ball!

But neither of us counted on the soaring temperatures that summer day, which started to melt my cake hat, attracting not only swarms of bees that followed me wherever

Me and Alarik looking like time travelers. The hand-lettered sign tied around my neck read HAPPY BIRTHDAY, AMERICA!

I went, but also drunk teenagers trying to lick my head. I had just recently had a bee fly down my underpants and sting me on my lady bits—I didn't need a head full of welts, too! But vanity prevailed. I wore that sucker all day and had teenagers and bees licking and stinging me wherever I went. Happy Tricentennial!

Hurricane season was always very exciting. We would batten down the hatches, fill the tubs with water, and bust out the kerosene lanterns. One year, a late fall hurricane brought the most amazing bounty. I was at Wilbur's buying a bag of Swedish fish when the daughter of a local lobsterman burst through the door and declared, "There's bears on Briggs Beach!"

Bears? I didn't even know there were bears in the State of Rhode Island. I had heard of whales on the beach. In fact, each year some poor whale carcass washes ashore. Those suckers are the size of a roller coaster. At first you go down to mourn the beautiful creature that got trapped in our little town, but then after a few days stuck on the beach in the sun, the smell of dead whale starts to permeate the village and they are so huge you can't move them. For a while people will try to be respectful and give the glorious whale the burial it deserves. Eventually everyone heads down to the beach with their small John Deere lawn riders and the farmers come with their backhoes and tractors, and they cover the poor guy in sand. For a few days, the shape of the beach changes and there will be a sand whale mountain that had not existed before. We are New Englanders; we adapt.

None of us ever considered rain. One good rain and all the burial sand is washed away, and then all you are left with is a sandy, ten-day-old stinky whale carcass waiting to greet the summer tourists.

"Welcome to your summer vacation! Hope you like the smell of putrefying Moby Dick at low tide!"

Eventually they have to hack up the poor guy and people come back with their John Deeres to bury the whale one tiny chunk at a time. (You'd think, in a town of pyromaniacs, someone would just blow him up.)

So when I heard there were bears on Briggs Beach, I was afraid. Were they alive and going to try to rip our heads off? Were there bear bodies all over the beach? Where did these beach bears come from?

Being a natural snoop, I hopped on my bicycle, threw caution to the wind, and sped off into the mist toward Briggs Beach. As I rounded the cove, I stumbled upon what can only be described as the beach version of Santa's workshop. As I approached, I saw there were bears covering the entire shoreline. Oh, there were bears everywhere—hundreds upon hundreds of them.

But these bears were teddy bears—plush toy bears of all sizes dressed smartly for fall in little navy and maroon argyle fisherman sweaters. Some of the toughest plumbers and fisherman in town were hooting and hollering and gathering up the bears into their booty bags. I never thought I would see Sully the Fisherman with his face lit up like a tween girl, giggling and stuffing teddy bears into a canvas sack. And that wasn't all of it—our town had finally gotten a mall! Albeit it was an outdoor, fishy-smelling mall for one day, but still.

Apparently, a large cargo shipping container headed for the discount store Bradley's had fallen off a barge and smashed into a rock near our harbor. The whole town had been turned into a department store overnight, and each of the beaches on our peninsula featured a different department.

The beach at the end of the Town Landing seemed to be the main footwear department. It was covered in white running shoes and the left shoes of many sets of navy ladies' evening high heels. In order to get the right shoe, you had to go down to the rocky beach by the river to the find its mate. Swap meets were set up in the school auditorium later in the week where people traded items—a ladies size 8 right shoe (navy) for a small bear, for instance.

The surfer's beach was the women's clothing department. Scattered on it were turtlenecks with little snowflakes and teal and magenta sweatshirts. Through the winter it was amazing to go for some Johnny Cakes (Rhode Island's version of a pancake made out of cornmeal) at the only restaurant in town and see tough dockworkers rocking hot pink snowflake turtlenecks. I have never seen anything manlier! Even Willy Myrin got his paws on a gigantic fuchsia pullover that he proudly wore to many a matinee. I tried to get him to give it to me.

"Willy, I'm pretty sure that is women's wear."

"Do I look like I give a shit? It was free. And you're just jealous you don't have one yourself!"

Driving around the day the bears washed ashore, it felt like the whole town was playing hooky. My friend Robin had her driver's license, and she squired me around town that day in her bright yellow Volkswagen Rabbit with 300,000 miles on it. We would pass groups of workmen riding around, standing in the back of pickups, cheering.

"Woo-hoo! This is better than Christmas!"

"Hell, this is better than sex!"

Our whole town had won the lottery! And Bradley's was cool with it—they were happy not to have to deal with the cleanup. The lucky and brave fishermen who dared boated out to the floating container and risked hauling themselves inside were rewarded handsomely. That was the holy grail of the unexpected bounty—the ELECTRONICS DEPARTMENT! Yes, inside floating shipping containers were not only classic brass and green glass desk lamps, but also full-blown TVs! It felt like Little Compton was in *Pirates of the Caribbean* and we had stumbled upon the Cave of Treasures! And all of it was free!

Everyone was included—if you could get to a beach, you could get free shit. Growing up with no malls, or even any stores in our town, made it that much more of a miracle. The Gods were finally rewarding Little Compton for years of fire worship and whale burials.

The last time I went to Little Compton I brought some of my friends from LA. Once they got over the fact that there was no cell service, they were entranced by that fact that coffee is sold in a tiny barn in an apple orchard, they jumped off cliffs into the ocean, and they even met Robert Mueller's brother (during the Mueller investigation) by accident at dinner. They were immediately ready to move there—every time you go to Little Compton, some magical, random thing happens. When you cross over the town line, it is like entering a time-travel portal. Just lock up your mail if you see a crow flying overhead.

The Awkward Years: Zero to Nineteen

For most of my youth I literally had a bowl cut. This was not out of some weird hipster fashion choice but because I did not like my hair to be washed, cleaned, or combed.

I also have twice the amount of hair on my head as a normal person has (the head of the *MADtv* hair department told me I could "wig a village"). My mom couldn't take the long, gnarled mess on my head, so out came the mixing bowl and a pair of scissors. JJ would plunk it on my head as she trimmed my hair around the bowl's perimeter. The result looked like a

Alarik, me, and my hair getting ready to go hide out at the fort in the woods.

red mushroom top had grown out of the crown of my head. Even as an elementary school child I knew that a head topped with ginger fungus would not do. I pleaded with my mom to get me a regular hairdo.

"Mom, *pleassssse*! I need to look alluring if I'm going to get discovered!"

She finally relented. There is only one act in

town to get your hair cut in Little Compton, and that is the local barber—appropriately named Tommy the Barber. Off JJ and I went for a little visit to see Tommy.

"Can you please cut her hair? She could make an ear bleed with the sounds she makes when I'm trying to cut it."

Tommy mostly cut the hair of all the fishermen in the village. He went to town with his clippers the only way he knew how—the official boys' buzz cut. So now I was a ten-year-old redheaded girl . . . with sideburns. I was also wearing knickers.

Oh yes, to go along with my Barb from *Stranger Things* look, I was also a very dapper dresser. While the cool girls in late '80s Rhode Island were rocking GUESS Jeans with zippers at the ankle and stripper feathers in their hair, my clothing style in sixth grade was 1830s Dickens orphan pickpocket. My prized possession was an itchy twill pair of knickers (think bloomers with a button below the knee to give maximum puffy effect around the knee and thigh areas) coupled with a herringbone wool vest and knee-high argyle socks. I looked like a gender-fluid ginger time traveler.

My mother was not really into buying me new clothes (most of my clothes were Alarik's hand-me-downs), but even she could not resist the lure of a jaunty pair of knickers. Janet sewed me a few different colors of knickerwear. Then I would put on my *Newsies* look and head off to conquer middle school! I reminded people of vintage photos of their immigrant grandfathers on the Lower East Side standing in front of a donkey pulling a cart of apples. I got high praise from my peers.

"You look like a museum doll."

On special occasions, we would drive to Massachusetts to go roller skating at Hot Wheels, a nearby rink, and I would wear my favorite bright purple corduroy party knickers for a Friday night on the town. While my peers seemed baffled by my dress of choice—"What the frick are you wearing?"—numerous parents would skate up to me and say, "I love your weird pants, young man." Victory!

I'm ready to party like it's 1899.

I was not the only one on Mr. Blackwell's Best Dressed list in my family. My brother Alarik has a head the size of a Volkswagen and the brains to fill it out. He was also the cutest toddler ever, sporting gigantic businessman glasses even as a three-year-old. Alarik was born blind in one eye, but he hasn't let that slow him down—he was running a computer programming company in his bedroom from the time he was ten, while I was busy making my Barbies hump in the yard.

Alarik's gigantic noggin came up with what may be the greatest accessory of all time—Sheetyhead. Until the age of five, my brother wore a fitted crib bed sheet on his head like a cape or a large bridal veil, which he called Sheetyhead. It was part security blanket, part best friend, full-time fierce fashion statement. Alarik could use Sheetyhead to fly, to hide, or be a ghost any time he wanted. It had the effect of a used, low-budget Halloween ghost costume.

The day my mother decided Sheetyhead was becoming a problem was the day she met up with her friend and former coworker Elaine at a zoo so they could introduce their two young

Alarik and Sheetyhead at the zoo.

sons to each other and have a playdate. My mom was excited to show off Alarik—his smarts, his charm, his personality. It did not go as planned.

Elaine's son, Jacob, was mesmerized by the zoo, going from cage to cage admiring all the animals.

"Wow! An elephant! Elephants are mammals, not marsupials!!!"

"That's right, Jacob! Alarik, which is your favorite animal?"

My brother was nowhere to be found. Later, my mom discovered him sulking in his cape near a picnic table.

"Why are there so many animals? Where are the slides?"

Eventually Alarik gave up looking for nonanimal entertainment and just rested his heavy head on the table, wrapping himself into a ball hiding under his sheet cloak while Jacob explored the monkey house alone. JJ was done with Sheetyhead. One day she "forgot it" on the ferry going to see Grandma. Alarik was devastated.

Clearly, the Myrin kids were not the coolest kids in middle school. The last summer of junior high I was starting to grow out my buzz cut to try to blend into the sea of ponytails that the other girls of eighth grade were wearing at the time. A few inches had already grown out, and I was feeling like maybe I could fly under the radar of the mean girls.

One afternoon after Alarik and I had exhausted ourselves watching *Love Connection* and kicking each other in the crotch to gain possession of the remote control, we called a truce and I entered my homegrown "day spa" portion of the day. My mom had recently gotten a new electric eggbeater. We loved it because we could whip up batch after batch of Duncan Hines cake mix and drink the batter straight from the bowl for an after-school treat. (The apple doesn't fall far from the cookie hammer tree.)

I was playing with the new eggbeater and was giving myself a nice head tickle by putting the whisks in my hair and hitting the whip button on the handle. (I always have been a sucker for having my back or head tickled. Lice checks in school were ecstasy for me! I would totally pay someone to come give me a daily lice check today just for the relaxing feeling of someone pawing through my scalp looking for nits.)

In any event, I was happily watching Chuck Woolery and whipping my hair into a froth when I realized the eggbeater had tangled up in my hair. I tried to pull the beater out and accidentally turned the mixer on high, whipping the eggbeater around my hair again and again. I ended up with a gigantic, tightly tangled knot of hair with an eggbeater stuck in it. It looked like a jellyfish made of hair tentacles had captured a kitchen appliance and clutched it tightly right to the front of my bangs area. JJ tried to remove it.

"Mom!! Get it out!!! Get it out! I can't start my last year of junior high with a cake mixer on my head!!"

"Calm down, peanut butter gets gum out of hair. We'll just put on a little peanut butter and it will be fine."

My mother rushed me and my eggbeater head into the kitchen and slathered it in Jif Creamy Peanut Butter. But still nothing was budging. I was sitting there covered in congealed hair knots, peanut butter, and eggbeater bangs.

"Rub harder, Mom, slather on more peanut butter."

Fingers full of peanut butter were scooped out and slathered onto my head, and rubbed around and around the appliance. And then it became clear. The beater was not going anywhere. Ever. Alarik could not stop laughing.

"You look like a total tool!!!"

Willy walked by and eyed the peanut butter on my head hungrily. I was cornered. There was no way this was going to end well. By then I was in a hysterical, teary frenzy; my mom had to calmly pin me down, pull out scissors, and chop out the entire chunk of bang hair, peanut butter, and egg beater. When it was all said and done I looked like the Chucky Doll from *Child's Play*.

Riddle for the reader: What *was* long and full and red all over, but became covered in peanut butter and cut in short spiky clumps right above the bang line? That's right, twelve-year-old Arden Myrin's hair about to head into eighth grade.

Thank you, God! I have never felt better! My confidence was high!!!!! Heading into eighth grade with the bangs of a serial killer, I was ready to go for it! Thankfully, middle school students are known for their kindness and welcoming acceptance . . .

Arden heading off to her first day of eighth grade.

"What happened to your head?! Did you get attacked by a dog?"

The worst part of eighth grade was that our history teacher, Miss McCall, had the class play a year-long role-playing game called Serfs and Landowners. The game involved drawing positions from a social caste out of a hat. For the whole year we would learn about survival and earning a living by playing our roles in society.

Basically, on day one, a slip of paper pulled from a Red Sox hat determined your fate for the year. Were you going to spend the year among the lucky few who got to be gentry or knights? Maybe you would really win the lottery and be a lord or lady—or even luckier, a king or a queen. Perhaps you would land squarely in the middle and be a town tradesperson, such as a cobbler or a leather worker, as most of the class did. Or maybe you would be one of the unlucky few who were forced to be a part of the lowest social caste, which was totally impossible to advance out of—aka serfdom.

Somehow the whole game seemed rigged. The popular mean girls all seemed to be queens or ladies in waiting. The rest of us—the monsters with the ginger buzz cuts—were their serfs. Needless to say, I was immediately made a serf. Was it the sideburns and mangled bangs that made me look like a person from a lower social caste? I'm sure the perma-knickers didn't help. I was purchased by my bitchy classmate Patty, who looked as adorable and innocent as Dr. Seuss's Cindy Lou Who but had a heart as black as pitch. Every day Patty would taunt me. "I own the land that you farm on. And I'm hungry! Start growing crops!"

Nothing like being assigned to a social caste commonly defined as modified slavery and being purchased by the worst child in America to really make the middle school experience a smooth and pleasant one.

Somehow I made it through the serf game, but surviving the day-in, day-out nightmare that is eighth grade was not a walk in the park. Gym class was especially torturous, as we were forced to play a homophobic version of dodgeball called Smear the Queer. Basically, one person was "The Queer" and everyone else had to pelt that person with red rubber balls. It was exactly the same as dodgeball but with an incredibly aggressive hate-crimey name.[8]

We also played with the Earth Ball—a gigantic ball seven feet in diameter that we would have to keep in the air, or else it would come smashing down and crush you as it pinned you to the earth.

But mostly gym class was torture because of Randy DeFazio, a former Marine drill sergeant the school hired as a gym teacher. Mr. DeFazio ran a tight ship. He was wowed by the chesty girls in my class (Sheryle heard him mutter, "Kristy's got a nice rack"), and he was horrified by me. He had never met a girl so loud or so flat chested.

---

8. Yes, that really was what it was called. It's still mind-boggling to me that just a few short years ago that was still an acceptable name for an elementary school gym class game. I have talked to other people who grew up in '80s, and they also called the game by this name at their schools.

"Take a chill pill, Ah-den!" he would scream at me as I spazzed out practicing my balance beam routine to a Janet Jackson song.

"My name ain't Baby! It's Arden. Miss Myrin if you're nasty!"

I was terrified of Mr. DeFazio. I went to a loosey-goosey Quaker[9] school where physical prowess was not a top priority. When Mr. DeFazio blew into the gym he would chomp on gum and twirl his whistle, making audible sounds of disgust watching our class. My brother had it worse, because on most days the boys and the girls were separated in gym class, and Mr. DeFazio presided over his male charges with an iron fist.

Alarik and I were both much, much smaller than the rest of our respective classmates. Randy gave Alarik an assignment— he had to go home and buy a cup.

My mother burst out laughing.

"Why? There isn't anything to protect."

A little harsh, but she had a point. These little dudes each weighed about fifty pounds. I don't think they were in much danger of doing permanent damage to the family jewels at that early stage of the game, but Mr. DeFazio had his priorities in order. Janet and Alarik headed off to buy him a cup.

Alarik returned with his cup and basically did his best just to avoid getting singled out in class. Wrestling was always a nightmare, as there was no one even close to Alarik's size that he could wrestle, but he would give it his all, wrestling the kid in his class who had asthma. The drill sergeant in Mr. DeFazio was appalled by how spoiled and lazy all the kids were at this Quaker grammar school.

---

9. Our school didn't actually practice or prescribe any religion, so I don't really know what made it Quaker (it was also known as The Society of Friends). Overall, it was a really welcoming, kind, and inclusive school. Aside from the gym class experience, I loved this school!

"You pussies disgust me. You are all a bunch of little wimps. Not one of you out there was being a real man. Actually, that's not true . . . there was one one of you little ladies who was really giving it his all."

Alarik started to panic.

Please don't say me. Please don't say me.

"Little Alarik My-REEN was out there. He may not be the biggest out there. Or the most athletic, or have the biggest nuts, but little Alarik My-REEN was going for it while you turds were tanning on the sidelines."

All the boys immediately glared at Alarik. He was horrified. He was done for. He was the chosen one of Randy DeFazio.

Alarik was tiny even though all he ate was Twinkies and SpaghettiOs. His palate expanded when our neighbors had a foreign exchange student from France, who we all laughed at in an incredibly xenophobic '80s way because he wore a fanny pack and was named François (François, if you're reading this, I'm so sorry!), but who we quickly befriended when we discovered his seemingly never-ending supply of Nutella.

At first, we mocked François's hazelnut spread; that is, until we dunked our greedy little fingers in the jar. Sweet Jesus! *Vive la France!!!* Alarik is not immune to the monster that lives inside him—he has the same sugar-craving beast that Willy and I have—and his beast got awoken by the joys of a hazelnut-chocolate food spread.

One night, Alarik and I were in the den with JJ watching the Miss America pageant. We always felt like underdogs because historically Miss Rhode Island never stood a chance against the behemoths from Texas or Mississippi. Rhode Island was usually the first voted out. But watching Miss America was like getting to watch our own sporting event. We loved to take bets on who would win and enjoyed the high-stakes danger of it. We would be glued to the television during the "talent" portion to see if a beauty queen would get smacked in the face by her baton.

That evening, Alarik had scored an entire unopened jar of Nutella from François that he proceeded to dive straight into with a spoon. No one batted an eye, as desserts and foods that were meant to be cooked or used as a spread were often ingested in their original form by a Myrin with a roving spoon. Cans of frosting, peanut butter, cake batter, cookie dough, and now Nutella were all fair game to spoon into our greedy little mouths, often leaving a beautiful batter mustache. At the time, Alarik was thirteen years old, four feet eleven inches, and weighed ninety-five pounds. Tops. (Think Anthony Michael Hall as Farmer Ted in *Sixteen Candles* and you'll get the picture.)

As Miss California was cleaning up in the bathing suit portion of the contest in her rockin' bikini, Alarik was quietly gobbling down spoon after spoon of the aforementioned nutty butter spread, and his mood was a little more surly than usual.

"California's got camel toe."

"No, she doesn't—that's a shadow."

"Whatever—you could park a car in her camel toe."

Alarik just kept spooning away. Nutella was an even richer substance than we were used to (it was so high in fat and so caloric it made cake batter look like diet food), but that didn't stop my brother. My mother didn't stop him either because he was so small she was just hoping that anything at that point would trigger a growth spurt—if not in height, then maybe in width.

"If you were Miss Rhode Island, you would have to wear a tankini."

"F you, Al!"

"Don't swear at your brother."

Alarik was busy growing a little hazelnut mustache and his mood was getting more aggressive by the minute. My normally sweet brother was turning into a hothead.

"You'd have to wear a full wet suit to protect the judges' eyes from melting."

"What?! You can't say that to people! That's super messed up."

"You didn't even finish your sleeve of Nutter Butters. Look at me! DONE!"

Wild-eyed, Alarik threw down the empty jar of Nutella—all 4,000 calories, 210 grams of sugar, and 114 grams of fat. His whole vibe seemed to suggest that he had started dabbling in crystal meth.

"Done! You loser! I finished!"

And then he didn't look so good. As Alarik's tiny body was trying to process this deluge of fat and calories, he started to weave around the room, turning gray as all the blood in his body rushed to his little tummy to try to break it down.

"Al, are you all right? You look like old lunch meat."

Alarik tore off toward the bathroom, where we heard retching noises followed by a crashing sound. Nutella had taken him down. He vomited. And then he blacked out. It turns out you can officially overdose on fancy French food.

Willy rounded the doorway when he heard the commotion and saw his son on the floor.

"What the hell happened to him?"

"Alarik ate a jar of Nutella, threw up, and then fainted."

"That's my boy! I was starting to think he was the milkman's son, but turns out he's mine!"

Crotch Chicken

Get out your Jergen's lotion and your high-speed rabbits, people! It's time to talk about sex. I appeared to take a very early interest in the subject. As a baby, whenever I was in the strapping arms of a hot-blooded American male, I would shamelessly bat my tiny eyelashes and wiggle my diaper at him like an incontinent Mae West. Appalled at his daughter's behavior, Willy would scream, "Get thee to a nunnery!" at his flirty infant.

My sexual education came in a very roundabout manner. As I never saw my parents kiss, much less share a couch or shake hands, I got a lot of my early information about sex from my best friend—television. Oh, how I loved TV!!!!!! Cool people lived on TV—people who resided in towns that had actual stoplights and real live shopping malls!

When I was a child, my mom and I watched *All My Children* every afternoon at 1 p.m. sharp. While the other kids in the neighborhood were outside climbing trees, I was indoors playing gin rummy and getting hot under my brother's hand-me-down collars, obsessively viewing the frisky sexploits of Erica Kane.[10] Mesmerized, I would stuff my face full of grilled cheese and Hawaiian Punch while sprawled out

---

10. Erica Kane, played by Susan Lucci, is THE GRAND DAME of daytime soap operas. She has been married and divorced like 93 times, had amnesia approximately 152 times, and is still foxy as hell.

on the hideous aqua blue wall-to-wall carpeting that covered our kitchen floor. From my perch, I'd soak up all the exciting, sexy promises of adulthood.

Watching *All My Children* made me impatient to be a grown-up, as I longed to live in Pine Valley and wear satin robes all day. I had a very elaborate fantasy life that revolved around when I would be old enough to have a hot gardener who would "stop by" while my husband was on a business trip. I would offer my guests brandy from a crystal decanter in between my murder cover-ups and my rendezvous with a set of twins, one who was hot and evil and the other who was like Forrest Gump and exclusively wore argyle cardigans. I couldn't wait to move into my TV!

Little Orphan Ardie and her pup Sandy!

We may not have had an overtly sexual household, but there was still plenty of sex happening in our home. I come from a long, proud line of dog humpers (dogs who love to hump people, not people who hump dogs), starting with our sheepdog Sandy, which was named after the dog from *Annie*. (Yes, I am the lamest person in America.) Sandy applied her skills as a herding dog, corralling me and my brother when we would get too wild brawling with each other all over the house. Racing in circles around the sharpest, least childproof coffee table on earth, Alarik and I would be hounded by a hairy beast nipping at our ankles. Eventually, Sandy would win by pushing us over and humping us into submission until we calmed down and behaved.

Our next family pet was a horny cockapoo named Mindy, a blind lapdog we got from the goalie of the New York Islanders. Surely a small dog wouldn't be able to dominate the household with her sexual demands! Wrong again. I am not sure what they teach dogs on the ice rinks of Long Island, but in Rhode Island that dog would go to town on my mother's ankle, humping it like her little life depended on it.

One night in fifth grade, my friend Sheryle braved a dinner with the Myrins. My brother and I were mostly focused on shoveling our SpaghettiOs into our mouths as fast as we could before Willy could eat it with his fingers. The TV was blaring, but even that could not drown out the sounds of grunting and panting coming from under the table. We did what we do well—pretended it wasn't happening. My family's motto should be "If you don't acknowledge something, it doesn't exist!"

My mother, ever the diplomat, tried to keep the conversation flowing.

"So, Sheryle, you'll be doing your gymnastics floor routine to 'Owner of a Lonely Heart'? Very progressive."

"Yes . . . I was torn between that and . . . "

Pant pant groan slurp . . . groan.

"I'm sorry—what is that noise?"

"Nothing."

I swallowed my gigantic mouthful of canned pasta and tried to intervene.

"Our dog has asthma. No biggie. So, what color unitard are you going to wear?"

Pant pant groan pant pant.

"I don't think your dog is okay . . . "

Before we could stop our guest, Sheryle looked under the table to find the groaning culprit: a glassy-eyed Mindy clasping for dear life onto my mother's leg as she humped the crap out of my mother's ankle.

"What is your dog doing??"

"Mom, tell her to stop!"

"Oh, let her have a little fun."

"I think I should probably go."

"Mom, please!"

I think Janet was secretly pleased that she had the most slim and alluring ankle in all the land.

"I can't help it that she favors my ankle."

Years later, we thought we had broken the curse of the humping dog, only to discover something far worse—a cocker spaniel named Rufus who would stroke your face with his paw, look deeply into your eyes, and try to French kiss you. I took a semester off from college and developed a very intimate relationship with that pup. Rufus was a very tender and affectionate face stroker but went bat-shit crazy whenever I went on a real date with a human being. He would shit all over the house, and I'd find him standing on the kitchen table, having ripped all of my mail and journals to shreds. Hanging out with that puppy was like dating Glenn Close in *Fatal Attraction*.

Having only pervy dogs and Susan Lucci to learn my sex facts from was confusing. It was clear that our dogs were having fun in the ole bathing suit area, and I could see that humans on TV were enjoying a romp in the hay, but I needed some cold, hard facts. Where were my birds and my bees?

Finally, when Alarik and I were old enough, an illustrated book called *What's Happening to Me?* was mysteriously left out on the dining room table. No one said anything. It just appeared one day. I squirreled it away to my closet to learn more. What a letdown. There were no sexy gardeners or hot twins with amnesia—just creepy drawings of kids going through puberty. The highlight of the book was an illustration of a pimply boy standing on the end of the diving board wearing a bathing suit and rocking a boner the size of a nuclear missile.

This book was the follow-up to the only other instruction I received: the literary classic *How Babies Are Made* by Andrew C. Andry and Steven Schepp. I'm pretty sure my mom got it at the thrift store. Our edition had faded photos of construction paper

Porn—Little Compton style!

cutouts of animals mating— think paper chickens humping other paper chickens. *Muy caliente!* I wasn't sure what a chicken giving a piggyback ride to another chicken had to do with what humans did in the bedroom, but I sensed that if so much was being hidden from me, it must be fun! I was on a mission to get more sex intel.

I wanted to know everything about sex, but no one was outright talking about it. I was already the town stripper. I didn't want to add "town deviant" to my résumé as well. You would think that having an older brother would have helped—it didn't. Alarik is not your average guy. He always claimed he was born with "no wild oats to sow," but I know that is not the case—I know because of a little game called "Crotch Chicken." Crotch Chicken is a game that Alarik made up, and he seems to be the only person in the world who has ever willingly entered into a match. Crotch Chicken operates much like a game of regular Chicken—except you use your hand to see how close you can get to another person's crotch. The first person to flinch loses. Probably best not to try this game outside your circle of family and friends!

When my best friends Katie and Sheryle would come over, Alarik the Perv would surface the second we entered his room.

"Crotch Chicken!! I'm gonna get your crotch!"

And before they knew it, this tiny, legally blind boy would be lurching his little hand toward their crotches with the goal of getting as close as he could before they flinched.

"Ew! Get your brother away from me!"

"Sorry, ladies. My room, my rules. I get to play Crotch Chicken."

I didn't have friends over a lot.

I decided to try playing Crotch Chicken and actually found that I enjoyed it. Whenever the UPS guy or our milkman would approach our door (yes, we had our milk delivered on a milk truck—I am a time traveler from the 1800s), my brother and I would race straight for the crotch.

"Crotch Chicken! Crotch Chicken! We're gonna get your crotch!"

"Are your parents home?"

"No, but your crotch is!"

When was I going to learn about sex for real? Crotch Chicken, paper chickens, and getting humped by four-legged animals just wasn't cutting it. In seventh grade my prayers got answered—it was finally time for sex-ed. Thank god I went to a very progressive, groovy Quaker school.

Somehow I got blessed with a teacher sent straight from the sex education gods—Mrs. H., a woman with a heavy Massachusetts accent who exclusively wore maroon leather blazers and smelled of cigarettes, coffee, and tuna fish. Mrs. H. was resplendent! But I felt bad for Mrs. H.—not only had she been given the unpleasant task of bringing the fifth-grade girls behind the curtain in the gym to show us videos about getting our breasts, but now she also had to teach the entire seventh-grade co-ed class about sex. I guess she had made up her mind: when teaching young students about sex, it was best to just cut to the chase.

God bless Mrs. H., for she did not disappoint. She plowed through all the basics: ovaries and herpes, the clap and sperm, ovulation and condoms. The content alone was enough to turn me into a quivering, giggling mess. Throw in her Boston accent and an incorrect pronunciation of the word *pubic*, and I was a goner.

"As you MAT-OOR you develop poobic hair on your poobic bone."

"Pooberty can begin as early as ten, when you might notice that you are growing poobs."

Poooooooooobs!

After Mrs. H. sped through the sanctioned syllabus, the real fun began. She took it up a notch when she decided to teach a class of thirteen nerds what she thought we *really* needed to know: oral sex, golden showers, and oh yes—Cleveland steamers.

"Some homosexuals[11] are aroused by urinatin' on one anothah. They also occasionally enjoy defecatin' on a glass surface above a mate's face."

WHAT???????? *People peeing on other people?! Are you KIDDING? That is what adults do?!* My mind was officially blown. That wasn't in my books. There was no construction paper bunny peeing on another paper bunny. Erica Kane never dropped trou and peed on Tad Martin. Forget it; I was DYING! I secretly started wondering if Mrs. H. was a freak in the sheets. All signs pointed to yes.

I was already a giggling mess hearing the words *semen* and *erections*, but you throw in these mind-boggling sex acts, and I LOST IT. I had never even held hands with a boy let alone kissed one, but now I was learning that some people preferred a little pepper in their pot when it came to sexual preferences. What was I going to do when I actually got a boyfriend? I was afraid that I might panic and go straight from hand holding to shitting on a glass plate over someone's face.

Clearly, Mrs. H. had high hopes for us in the bedroom. Sex-ed class wasn't the only thing pressuring me to get a move on in the sack—JJ was so paranoid about me getting pregnant that the day she noticed my breasts were "budding," she told me

---

11. As an adult, I realized how ridiculous this was. Most gay men I know are much more gentlemanly than straight guys! Sure, some love a leather bar and a hairless torso, but they also keep beautiful apartments, are interested in going antiquing, and love a *RuPaul's Drag Race* marathon. In my experience, it's the repressed straight guys who are the biggest deviants. Hello?! *Two Girls One Cup*, anyone?

that I could go on the pill whenever I wanted and put a cup of condoms on my dresser. I did not want to disappoint! My mom was like a Tennessee Williams character who wanted me to have a "man in every port." I thought that sounded like a great idea and was totally game to be the town hussy. I was ready to become a bobcat in the sack, but I had to start with actually kissing a boy first.

Fortunately, I was a stunning beauty in junior high!

Oddly, at the time, the flat-chested knicker-wearing ginger look wasn't in. It didn't matter—I was on a mission to find a

The belle of the junior high ball.

boyfriend, and if he was a bad boy, even better. The object of my affection? An eighty-pound skate rat named Scott. Hello, raging danger! I knew Scott was my boyfriend because he called me up and said, "You wanna go out?" I don't think we ever spoke again. It was the perfect relationship.

I had finally gotten a boyfriend, but apparently I could not bully him into a kiss. Sheryle and I would set up fake movie chair situations where we would practice trying to position ourselves to be the most available and alluring to encourage a nice, healthy landing place for a smooch. We would practice the subtle arm touch—a throw pillow between us standing in for the armrest in our grimy local theater.

Because the movie theater was a half hour away, I had to settle for movie night at Scott's house. I knew it was *on* when Scott invited me over to watch *The Shining* on his VCR. Clearly,

he had romance on his mind, and I was determined to get
my first kiss. I wanted to pull out all the stops: offer him some
brandy from a decanter; show him some of my fancy cutout
paper chicken moves; at the very least, let him know I was in the
throes of *pooberty*. But when push came to shove and I finally got
my kiss, it was exactly as it should be—two thirteen-year-olds,
two sets of braces, and Jack Nicholson in the background losing
his mind over creepy twins and rivers of blood. Nothing could
have been more appropriate.

* * *

Medical and Dental: The Myrin HMO!

YOU ARE THE CEO OF YOUR OWN BODY. XO, JJ

I had just woken up to this text from my mom, and I was under the weather. What did she want me to do? Dress like Steve Jobs in a black turtleneck and talk to my body TED Talk style? *I just need to Power Pose, and my immune system will be impenetrable!*

I think this was JJ code telling me to speak up for myself more when I went to the doctor. There was only one problem: I have always had a crippling fear of going to the doctor, and more specifically, a fear of needles. I always felt like this fear would go away as I got older. Not so! I am just as freaked out now as I was as a young child. However, I think watching my dad's disregard for his body was a good cautionary tale of what *not* to do.

Willy hadn't gone to the dentist in twelve years when he finally went at the age of forty. As you would expect, he had more than a few cavities. This man's forward thinking in response to the prospect of coming face to face with a drill was truly mind-boggling. Rather than go get his teeth filled, my father decided right then and there to just rip them all out.

That's right—my dad rocked a full set of dentures for almost half his life. Not caps, not crowns—DENTURES. Who does that?! Who chooses to remove ALL THEIR TEETH rather than deal with them at forty? Being over the age of forty now really puts into perspective for me how young he was and just how crazy and defiant a move that was. As a kid, forty seemed so old that I just accepted that that was what all adults do. But now, it is shocking to me that he treated his body this way.

"Best thing I ever did!" he claimed.

He tried to get me to rip my teeth out, too.

"Why bother dealing with them if at some point you're going to have to rip them out anyway? Save yourself the heartache and the money."

I have to admit, he did have a point. But I wasn't about to let that become my *thing*, my signature flair. She's sassy, she's toothless, and she's ready to party!

That is also a super gnarly way to treat your body.

Willy managed to use his dentures like an amazing party trick. As an adult I was once chatting on the phone with my dad while my brother was paying him a visit.

"How you doing, Willy?"

All I could hear was a crashing sound and my brother in the background shouting, "Holy Christ!"

"Is everything okay?'

"I just gave your brother a stroke."

At which point my brother grabbed the phone to relay what had happened. Turns out Willy was attempting to give me a raspberry (as most seventy-year-old men normally do) but didn't remember that he had not secured his teeth that day. As he started to raspberry, his teeth rocketed out of his mouth and across the room, much to my brother's horror.

Witnessing the man who gave me half of my DNA treat his body so flippantly was the ultimate wake-up call for me to start taking care of myself. When I moved to Los Angeles, the first thing anyone wanted to do was recommend doctors to me. LA is a city filled with so many hypochondriacs that people panic even if they are talking to you *on the phone* and you sound off at all.

"Do you have a cold? Oh my god. You have a cold. You *really* sound stuffed up. You need to go see my chiropractor!"

"For a cold?"

People in LA go to chiropractors for everything. I got talked into going to one once for a jacked-up neck, but it seemed like the man was just interested in cracking my pelvis. No thank you. I don't think that is where I am holding my tension, Dr. Perv.

I would like to stop going to the doctor altogether, but I can't amputate all my limbs, so sadly, for now, I must keep going. Unfortunately, I am very accident-prone. I mostly have had very painful, and painfully embarrassing, injuries. I have burned my eyeball with a curling iron, smashed my hand in a handicap bathroom door on an Amtrak train (a silver "fingernail" was sewn on to one fingertip to keep the nailbed open as it healed), and I've broken my vagina while doing the Worm. But more on that later.

I have a very complex relationship with going to the doctor: on the one hand I hate it, and on the other hand I *really, really* hate it. My grandma Hilda was a Christian Scientist, and I enjoyed her antidoctor approach to medicine. She came by it honestly—when she was a young girl, she developed polio, and modern medicine failed her. She was a strong, vivacious lady, despite the fact that one of her legs was much smaller than the other as a result of her childhood disease. She never made a fuss about it and reminded me of Katharine Hepburn as she swam in a creek outside her door every summer morning.

Whenever anything requiring medical attention happened to me or my brother under her watch, she would throw us into salt water. Got a cold? Go for a swim in the ocean! Broken limb? Breast stroke it out! That pesky case of walking pneumonia getting you down? Nothing a little January dip in the Atlantic can't help.

Thankfully, most of the terrible maladies that run in my family are self-inflicted. No one is going to tie you down and force you to eat two sticks of butter and a sheet cake or force you to smoke a pack of Lark cigarettes[12] every day, washed down by a handle of gin.

In general, the Myrin family is pretty no-nonsense when it comes to health and big life events. They have a real stiff-upper-lip quality that I really admire but which is totally lacking in me. To say my family downplays an illness is an understatement—if you actually hear about someone being sick, you know it is baaaaad. Like time-to-call-in-a-priest bad. And I appreciate that.

My family doesn't like to burden others with bad news. They don't want to upset your day. My grandfather had been sick, and I called his house to check up on him one morning. JJ answered the phone.

"Grandpa can't talk."

"Oh . . . is he sleeping?"

"Grandpa is more than sleeping."

"He's napping really hard?"

"No—he's dead."

I found out that my mom had cancer when she told me on the phone—*after* she told me three other items of local gossip.

---

12. I have never seen this brand of cigarettes anywhere on earth except on my father's nightstand. He may very well have been their only customer.

"Clare bought a new yak, Susan Fortmiller is getting divorced, someone knocked down our stone wall with a bat, I have a little bit of cancer, and I am thinking of adding a skylight to the living room."

"I'm sorry, what was fourth on your list?"

"Some kids hit our wall with a baseball bat?"

Thankfully, Janet's cancer scare was caught early, but at the time, she dealt with her "little bit of cancer" in her stiff-upper-lip manner. She booked her hysterectomy for a morning, went back to work in the afternoon, and made a joke to my friend Katie that she could use her uterus as the casing for a new Bermuda handbag..

Being Janet Myrin's daughter makes it extra embarrassing that I am such a total wuss at the doctor. I wish I had my mother's disposition. Whereas she was practical, calm, and cool, I am a disaster. A sissy and the devil rolled together make one freak of a human.

The popular '80s purse—the Bermuda bag—had covers you could swap out.

For starters, I travel to a doctor's appointment with stacks of trashy magazines and a pile of blankets to recreate a sort of low-budget weighted blanket to calm my nerves during my exam.

I pile the blankets on top of my body on the exam table and bury my nose in *In Touch* magazines. When the nightmare that is my annual Pap smear occurs, I use my mighty, magical, lower-body Corgi strength to scoot up the table—slowly but surely—away from the mighty prying eyes of my gynecologist and his violating speculum.

I make weird jokes and panic and try to distract him from the task at hand.

"Find anything good in there?"

"How do you think those ladies shoot those Ping-Pong balls so far out of their lady parts at that show in Bangkok?"

"Did you hear the rumor that Paris Hilton once got caught hiding cocaine in her vagina? Her snooch must be the size of a U-boat."

I try this hacky material on the off chance that maybe my doctor will forget he is a gynecologist. Maybe he will think this is just some bad date. When his cell phone rings with his "Take Me Out to the Ball Game" theme song, I take the occasion to slither back up the table—only to be dragged back down with my blankets and fleeces and *In Touch* magazines piled high on top of me like an igloo. Yes, my gyno's ringtone is "Take Me Out to the Ball Game."

That is because my gynecologist is a former third baseman for the Mets. For real. I wouldn't let anyone who had not played ball in Queens be trusted with keeping my baby maker safe!

He is not my first celebrity doctor. Strangely, all my doctors have turned out to have been kind of famous in their former lives.

My very first doctor was a lovely and patient local physician in Little Compton. He also happened to be Dr. von Trapp, the eldest child of the real-life *Sound of Music* von Trapps. As in "The Hills Are Alive with the Sound of Julie Andrews" von Trapps. No, Liesl von Trapp was not my pediatrician. Rupert von Trapp was.

Not ringing a bell? Rupert was the real-life eldest child of Captain von Trapp. He sang with his siblings in matching outfits made out of drapes and crossed the Alps to freedom to escape the Nazis—but even with all that under his belt, poor Rupert *still* did not exist in the movie. My mind is still blown at the injustice of it! Even doing *one* of those things should have warranted at least a cameo. Rupert wasn't included in the plot because Hollywood had literally turned him into a girl—Liesl. Was it that much better of a narrative to have a beautiful girl who is sixteen going on seventeen falling in love in a rain-drenched gazebo with Rolf, the horrible whistle-blowing Nazi? Couldn't Rupert have "played doctor" with a couple of the cuter nuns? I would have watched *that* movie.

As much as I hated going to the doctor, I was obsessed with my proximity to my very first celebrity. So what if Dr. von Trapp wasn't even included in the movie? That's just a technicality. Going in for my annual checkups I always felt a mixture of terror and being starstruck. JJ would throw me in the way back of her huge station wagon and drive me down the hill to his office that was in a massive, old, white Colonial house.

It was horrible because I knew this celeb would see me at my most charmless. As a child (and as an adult) I would screech and scream and race around the exam room whenever it was time to get a shot. Even as a four-year-old, I was a terrible, weird little patient. As I mentioned, I have a lifelong crippling fear of needles. Now couple that with an embarrassingly desperate need to entertain. While getting shots, it would take two nurses to pin me down like the girl in the *Exorcist*. (Today I still do Lamaze breaths while getting my blood pressure taken and then faint when the tiniest amount of blood is drawn. I flatter the nurses with false compliments, hoping they will take pity on me and set me free. "You sure do look pretty! White clogs are hard to pull off!") As I was being driven to Dr. von Trapp's office, I would repeat mantras to myself.

"Today I am going to behave! I am going to act like a normal person. I'm not going to ask stupid questions about *The Sound of Music*."

Within twenty seconds of entering the office, I was off and running, a total freak show.

"How do you do, Doctor von Trapp? Did Maria really have such a lame haircut? Do you still have the marionettes? If you give me a shot, I'll bite you!"

Dr. von Trapp was the savviest of all my celebrity doctors. He would calm me down with the oldest trick in the book—the promise of candy.

"Hello, Arden. Why don't you and I have a lollipop together and just chitchat?"

Then sneaky, magical Dr. von Trapp would pull out a jar of Dum-Dums.

Immediately, I would be lulled into a trance by the sight of sugar (I am my father's daughter, after all). Like a candy zombie, I would walk over to the kindly von Trapp with my arm outstretched, mesmerized by the treat.

"Lolli . . . looooollllii . . . must have lollipop."

As my hand neared the lolly, he would jam a shot into my arm. *WTF?!!??*

Liesl wouldn't have done that to me! I was furious, but delighted he let me keep the candy. It was hard to hold a grudge; my love of sweets and celebrities overrode my fear of vaccinations.

Once I realized that not all doctors bribe you with sweets, I made up my mind that I would never, ever go to a medical professional again. However, I didn't take into account the fact that I am extremely accident-prone. Just a few years ago I almost died from a blood clot. A blood clot in my crotch. A blood clot that I procured while doing the 1980s dance move the Worm during a comedy show. See? I told you I would come back to this! There are two things that I love in life: I love comedy, and I love to dance. Sometimes these two things merge into one and have life-threatening results.

I was at a comedy show when the classic and elegant Bell Biv DeVoe hit song "That Girl Is Poison" came on during another performer's act. Before you can say "Never trust a big butt and a smile!" I was touched by the fever of the dance gods. I threw myself to the ground and began furiously doing the Worm across the stage behind the other performer. (Nothing upstaging about that.)

The crowd did not go wild.

The accident happened after I had safely wormed my way to the other side of the stage and realized there was no place for me to hide. Rather than just hold my head high and walk back quietly to the backstage area, I tried to subtly worm my way back across the stage to safety. No such luck. On my return trip, I accidentally wormed over a metal microphone cord.

I knew I was in trouble when I went to the ladies' room and found that a big black blowfish had moved into my pants. One side of my vagina looked like it normally does and could have played the part of Hermione in *Harry Potter*, and the other side looked like I had sewn an eight ball onto my crotch.

I couldn't pull a "Willy at the dentist" and just have my vagina removed, so I had to actually go seek medical attention. I went to see Dr. Andy Baseball. If he could catch a ball going ninety miles an hour, he could deal with this sensitive situation on my lady bits.

Dr. Andy Baseball really sets the scene. He has artwork of topless women and sculptures of naked women breastfeeding their children all over his office. He also has a tough, no-nonsense nurse named Mandy who chats with me about my career when my feet are in stirrups and I'm in the middle of a Pap smear.

"You know why *MADtv* wasn't as good as *SNL*? Not enough recurring characters."

When Andy and Mandy saw what was in my pants, they both flinched. That is never a good sign.

"What happened to you?"

"I was worming."

They looked at me like I was speaking in tongues.

"You know, the Worm? I did it and this happened."

"Why would you do that?"

I was in my thirties, my legs were in the stirrups, and I had a huge-half black vagina. I just panicked and screamed, "Because I still got it!!"

No, my friend. You don't. You don't still "got it." Not like that.

I am sure Andy and Mandy have seen every creepy thing that could happen to a lady's crotch in Southern California, but mine appeared to be one for the record books. That is not the kind of record breaker I wanted to be—Arden Myrin: Most Broken Crotch in Hollywood. But you have to admit, that takes some hard work.

Little did Chelsea know: I had a broken snooch during the panel!

Andy and Mandy were worried that I might die. I had given myself a legitimate blood clot. My prescription was as follows: I had to sit and ice the blood clot every night for an hour. While the rest of LA was out hobnobbing, I was sitting at home, pantsless, with a big bag of frozen blueberries on my crotch, watching reruns of *Little Women: Atlanta.* If I felt dizzy, I was to go immediately to the ER. Unfortunately, I was booked to do the roundtable on *Chelsea Lately* the next day.

Because I am an idiot, when I arrived at *Chelsea Lately* (wearing a much looser-than-normal "sister wife"–type skirt), I confided what had happened to Chelsea's brother, Roy.

"I'm nervous to go on the air, Roy. I could die."

Roy looked at me blankly and said, "If you did drop dead from a gigantic swollen vagina that you gave yourself from doing the Worm, Chelsea would make so much fun of you on the air. You would be the greatest roundtable topic ever."

He laughed in my face and walked away.

And that was when I knew that I was in the right place.

Wine-NO!

Know your limits, kitty cats! I have social anxiety. Other people scare me. They seem so put together and confident and comfortable in their skin. I still get a little nervous when I have to socialize with people, but over the years I have practiced venturing out of my comfort zone. I don't want to be the Boo Radley of the block. Fake it 'til you make it, honey—but watch out for pitfalls! I want to be able to hang with elegant people—people who eat figs and drink Prosecco and listen to *Pod Saves America*. But that is not my natural habitat. If you are forced to socialize with fancy, well-read people, when in doubt, breathe, ask questions, try to make eye contact, and don't accuse the host of giving you food poisoning. Most important, wine may seem like your friend, but *beware the endless bottle of wine*. I learned this the hard way.

My friend Katie Whitman's family always seemed like the opposite of my family. I met Katie sophomore year in high school, and I was wowed by her, but that was a drop in the bucket compared with my awe of the whole House of Whitman. I had never seen anything like how the Whitmans lived. Their whole world looked like a Wes Anderson set, while ours looked like *Married . . . with Children*, but with June Cleaver stepping in for Peg Bundy.

I loved going over to the Whitman's house. My family had a VHS copy of the movie *Ski Patrol*, a kitchen that was carpeted with aqua blue wall-to-wall carpeting (which was excellent to take naps on with our family sheepdog), and an aging bologna sandwich on top of our fridge. The Whitmans had a cello room, books (without pictures in them), and exotic bohemian rugs from their world travels. NPR was always playing during the Whitman's dinner of home-cooked roast chicken and pies made from scratch. They were the first family that fed me balsamic vinegar and arugula—they were classy!!

However, while their meals were elegant, I was confused by their food offerings. Where was the iceberg lettuce with canned pears and Catalina dressing? (A special holiday salad treat chez Myrin.) What was with all the homemade pesto? Could they not afford Ragu?

Katie's parents were both doctors and had a library filled with leather-bound copies of the *New Yorker* (not just aging *TV Guide*s) that they actually read. I wanted to move in with this family and have them adopt me and treat me like a precocious orphan they had taken under their wing. They could teach me about traveling in Peru, and I could teach them about who Zack Morris was on *Saved by the Bell*.

The best part of the Whitmans was that they were the first people to treat me like the elegant young lady that I was and let me have wine with dinner. I was seventeen years old when Katie invited me over for a delicious dinner of Cornish game hens. I was seated at the table with Katie, the good doctors, Katie's sister Rachel, and their intellectual cousins. The wine was getting passed around, and I was honored that they filled my glass up without any fuss. How European! Katie and Rachel seemed nonplussed and didn't make a big deal about the wine, so who was I to turn away free libations? I had never had wine before, but how bad could I behave in a house full of cellos? "News from Lake Wobegon" was playing in the background. I laughed when they laughed, listening to Garrison Keillor. I didn't get it; it seemed a little *booorrring*, but who cares? I was drinking WINNNEEEEEEEEEE!!!!!!

Finally, I was among people who would appreciate my specialness. I could pretend I was Sofia Coppola and that I just loved to eat olives and discuss kayaking.

"I've always wanted to own a loom!" I blurted out to no one in particular. I was blending right in. So far, so good.

Silence.

"As I was saying, a patient of mine . . . "

At first, the taste of wine was not that fantastic, but the warm deliciousness was kicking in and suddenly made the special grape juice the greatest drink I had ever consumed. I was soon feeling loose and sophisticated and dove headfirst into the conversation, attempting to bond over their chosen professions.

"Speaking of medicine, my grandmother is a Christian Scientist. I know. You don't have to tell me. Loco in the coco, am I right?"

I wanted to make it a perfect evening, so I leaned over and whisper-slurred hotly in Katie's ear.

"When do we get to watch TV?"

"We don't have a TV."

"I'm sorry . . . WHAT????!!!"

I wanted to scream, "No TV?!!! What the FUCK????? What is wrong with you people? What do you do for fun? Who babysits you? Who is your most tried-and-true friend in all the land?"

As I've told you, Myrins have had a long love affair with television. When I first moved to Chicago at nineteen, before my mother dropped me off in my studio apartment complete with a Murphy bed, she took me to Marshall Fields and bought me a thirteen-inch TV.

"Now you can't complain that you don't have any friends."

My mom was right. She did buy my friends (who were thirteen inches tall).

With no TV to mesmerize the crowd, I didn't know what we were going to do for the rest of the night. Talk to each other? Listen to them play concertos on stringed instruments? Before I could suggest we borrow a TV from my family, Katie's mom said, "Let's play some after-dinner parlor games!"

Okay, odd call. Didn't see that coming. But I was into it—I love me a game. I wasn't sure what a parlor game was, but with my new friend wine coursing through my system, I was certain any game would be a fun one. One weird gift I have is being oddly good at card games and board games. I knew if we played games, at least I would be able to strut my stuff with these intellectuals. I wanted them to like me, but I felt kind of sorry for them—they didn't know the ringer that was about to descend on their little "parlor game."

I was bred to be a card shark from an early age. Janet's mother, Hilda (the sassy Christian Scientist herself!), was a ruthless card player who ran a tight ship at the card table. Hilda didn't take it easy on you just because you were five. The summer after kindergarten one could frequently hear the following getting shouted at me across a lazy Susan filled with doilies, Cheetos, Wild Turkey, and cards:

"Chest your cards!"

"If you were going to try to shoot the moon, you should have wondered where the ace of hearts was, Arden!"

"A card laid is a card played!"

"A card laid is a card played" was browbeaten into me from the time I was four, when I graduated from *Go Fish* to playing *Hearts* with Grandma Hilda and her friends. When I would hem and haw about putting a card down, the second my little hand left the card I would hear Grandma Hilda screaming, "A card laid is a card played, little one! Make a choice and stick with it!"

(Grandma Hilda's decisive card-playing tactics made it odd to me that she was not one of the founding members of the Hasty Decisions Club, although she did announce: "That's the man I am going to marry!" five minutes after meeting my grandfather Harry for the first time.)

Card shark training came right after cocktail hour every night. Cocktail hour was 5 p.m. sharp, when my grandparents would put out bowls of Cheetos and Chex Mix next to some cheddar. We were classy, too! Hilda and Harry would bust open the Wild Turkey, and the festivities would begin. Even though my grandpa was always seated right by her side, my grandma had a genius way of getting him to do her bidding.

"While you're up, Harry, could you get me some more Wild Turkey?"

Harry was never "up," but he was a good guy and would hop to his feet and get his lady another cocktail. I never saw my grandma drunk—she was four feet eight inches of pure wooden leg.

Grandma also had a habit of reading the *New York Times* every day and would grill the grandchildren about current events. Once, during the mid-nineties, while all the grandchildren were sitting around, she singled me out: "Arden, have you ever tried crack cocaine?"

My brother was overjoyed.

"Yeah, Arden, have you ever tried crack cocaine?" Alarik stammered out while giggling and guffawing.

"No! I have not."

And I did not appreciate being nominated as the grandchild "Most Likely to Be a Crackhead."

Alarik couldn't let such a golden moment die and decided to throw another question my way.

"Have you smoked pot, Arden?"

From across the porch my mother was glaring at me, waiting for my answer. The lame thing was I was about to get busted for something I didn't even like when I tried it. Why couldn't he have asked, "Arden, have you ever eaten a whole pie?"

"Well, I've *tried* pot . . . but it's not really my cup of tea."

"And there you have it, ladies and gentlemen! My sister has tried pot. I think that explains a lot, don't you?"

My brother had become some kind of John Grisham-esque trial lawyer, and it had to stop.

"Have you ever jacked off in the coat closet, Alarik?"

I got grounded for a week. I suppose it's best not to use the phrase "jacked off" in front of a grandparent, *even if* you have just been accused of being a crackhead. Regardless, I was spared by Hilda; she liked me because I could hold my own at the card table.

When Dr. Whitman pulled out *Go to the Head of the Class*, I thought, "You have got to be kidding me! That's a baby's game." After all, it was for ages seven and up. This was gonna be a cakewalk. I was also impressed that these sophisticated people would slum it with a game that I had played when I was five. How highbrow-lowbrow!

We all lined up our pawns on our little desks on the cardboard classroom. I hadn't played *Go to the Head of the Class* since second grade but figured it might be fun with my very first wine buzz.

It soon became crystal clear that I was out of my league when the first question began with, "Which Founding Father . . . " *Oh no.* This was no ordinary version of *Go to the Head of the Class.* Noooo! This smarty family had a weird "Graduate Edition" I'm sure they bought in some Learning Is Fun! PBS toy store filled with wooden blocks and home-schooled patrons.

"Who arrived at the Constitutional Convention in a sedan chair carried by prisoners?"

What the hell kind of question was that? They all started shouting at once.

"Benjamin Franklin!! Benjamin Franklin!!"

"That one was easy!"

I tried to chime in. "Wow! Who would have thought they had sedan chairs—" But I was cut off. The game train had left the station and everybody was on board but me.

"What American senator was attacked with a cane in the days before the Civil War?"

Who wrote these creepy questions?

"Charles Sumner!! Charles Sumner!!"

I had never been with a group of people that took gaming so seriously and were so good at it. And knew real facts.

"Arden, your turn."

I just prayed that I got an entertainment question. I wanted to wow my hosts. What was with all the early American history questions? I do better when trivia has to do with the history of the cast of *RuPaul's Drag Race*: "Did you know Raja was originally a makeup artist on *America's Next Top Model*!?"

I rolled the dice. *Shit.* "Geography."

"Okay, here's an easy one. What is the capital of Zambia?"

"Um . . . hmmmm . . . Zambia? Can I hear it used in a sentence, please?"

"Here's a sentence: Arden doesn't know the capital of Zambia."

Eyes darting; smirks.

I was not amused. I decided to have more and more glasses of the yummy wine to soften the blow of this horrible devil's game. Delicious!! As the night wore on, I may not have been advancing in the classroom, but my purple wine mustache had advanced on my upper lip from pencil thin to a full Tom Selleck *Magnum, P.I.* 'stache.

I got a little slurrier and slurrier.

"Whyyy don' we play *Go Fish?* Here fissshchy fischy fisshchy . . . "

"No! We're playing *Go to the Head of the Class.*"

These people were sadists. Didn't anyone know there was a *brand-new* episode of *Beverly Hills 90210* on? Was Donna Martin finally going to lose her virginity to David Silver, or was bad boy Pumpkin Boy Ray "How Do You Talk to An Angel" Pruitt going to steal her maidenhood?

Had this stupid game asked me about the urban myth about Tori Spelling's audition to play Donna Martin, I totally could have scored points: Tori went in under a pseudonym, dressed as someone else—no one *knew* it was Aaron Spelling's daughter. She won the part on her own merit! I could have moved a few desks ahead for that, but *nooooo.* It was all facts, facts, facts! More wine, please!

As the game wore on, the competition got fiercer. These intellectuals were not messing around with their *Go to the Head of the Class*. In a matter of moments, I was in kindergarten while the rest of my competitors zoomed ahead to eighth grade, with a mad dash for the finish line. Katie's doctor parents were clearly people who excelled in higher learning institutions and didn't go to Puerto Rico on a dare in a cargo plane full of fighting chickens during their college's *final exam week*—like my dad did during his last week enrolled in college. It was his last week enrolled in college because he got kicked out for *flying to Puerto Rico on a dare*.

"Biology. What physical symptom is exhibited by those who suffer from blepharospasms?"

"Ummm . . . they belch a lot?"

"No. Uncontrollable winking."

I burst into laughter and started winking uncontrollably at the doctors.

They were not amused. I supposed winking at your friend's parents is never a good idea. Sober or drunk.

That was it for me. I had to save some face. I slurred out, "Can't we play some cardsssss? I am sssooo good at cards."

"Fine. We'll play cards. For Arden. Everyone remember where their pawn was so we can play tomorrow."

They could play without me. I was fine with that because it was card time, y'all!! Cards are my thang! At least I could show them I wasn't a total idiot. After the hateful board game debacle, I thought I was in the clear until Rachel suggested a card game called Pounce. Everyone seemed excited about it—a little too excited.

"Yes! Pounce! Pounce!!!"

Sounded like another baby game. I had never played Pounce and was a little tipsy but was pretty confident that I could rock it out and show these genetically superior freaks who was boss, because Grandma Hilda had schooled me in all sorts of card games. By the age of eight I was an adept poker and gin rummy player. We had a little poker set, and Hilda would run the table. I learned Texas Hold'em in a trial by fire when the rest of my friends were playing *Hungry Hungry Hippos. And* their kindly relatives would let them win.

By the age of nine I was a poker addict. I would go to my friends' houses and start out with a boring game of *Go Fish*, gradually suggesting that I could teach them how to play poker. I would then pull out my sticker collection and innocently suggest using stickers or jewelry beads as our chips. My prey agreed that that sounded like a great idea, and before you knew it I had grifted my friends of their treasures. I was in possession of the greatest sticker and bead collection in the Northeast by the time I was eleven. I was sure their precious Pounce would not be a problem for me.

The game of Pounce is much like the game of solitaire, only played against other people. Everyone has their own deck of cards, and the first person to use their entire deck slaps one of the discard piles in the middle and screams, "Pounce!" Easy enough.

Katie handed out the decks, and everyone had their lucky deck that, clearly, they had been playing with for decades. There was a deck with Clydesdales on them, literary cards with Jane Austen characters, and classic old-school Bicycle Playing Cards in navy and red. I was used to playing with cards from Spencer

Gifts that had boobs on them, but cards are all the same on the other side, boobs or no boobs.

Everyone shuffled and laid out their cards, and the game began. It was chaos! It felt like I was standing on the floor of the stock exchange. Action was happening at lightning speed around me and I was the idiot slowly counting my cards.

"One, two, three, flip . . . "

I was trying to focus and get back in the game when I heard a weird rumbling sound. It was sort of a murmur, but then I figured out it was the oddest version of trash talking that I had ever heard. This elegant family was doing a combo of aggressively muttering to themselves while insulting one another, and me.

"I'm gonna get you . . . you think you're all that, but I am going to *pounce* and rip your face off."

"Pounce-a-dee, pounce. Who's the little mouse? You are, Arden! And you just got devoured by the cat—fool!!!!"

What was going on??? Where do doctors learn how to trash talk? I had barely put a card down when Katie's mild-mannered sister slammed her victorious open palm down with hurricane force.

"Pounce! Pounce! You just got pounced, suckers! Did I blow your mind?!"

She did blow my mind. I had never been so outplayed at so many games. This was turning into the worst night of my life, wine or no wine.

When someone suggested we go swimming, I couldn't have been more relieved. I had never been so schooled at the game table in my life. Katie's parents went to bed after being vicious competitors yet were incredibly gracious hosts for the entire evening. With Katie's parents off cuddling up, Katie, Rachel, the educated cousins, and I headed off into the night. I had not won a single hand, but I had won my first wine buzz.

Secretly I had been topping off my wine all night. I probably had swilled a full bottle of wine, and nothing seemed like a better drunk idea than going night swimming. I was exhausted from having been a wonderful dining companion and intellectual heavyweight during *Go to the Head of the Class*.

The "swimming" was actually jumping off a bridge from an overpass into a shallow river. (Yes, in fact I will follow my friends if they jump off a bridge.) Perhaps not the wisest thing I have ever done.

It's a funny thing when you are naturally a silly, noisy girl; most of the time people assume you are drunk anyway. When I actually am drunk, I get sleepy and quiet. My friend calls it the hummingbird syndrome. I go a million miles an hour, and then I'm just *done*. Crashed. I get a little narcoleptic. While everyone else was bravely jumping into the water, I got very sleepy. Stained purple like Violet Beauregarde, I slithered from the riverbank into the tide and sat quietly giggling in ten inches of water while everyone else played around me.

When we got back from our big night and as everyone else was settling in to sleep, I suddenly didn't feel so well. I ran to the bathroom and proceeded to violently throw up a steady stream of purple wine rainbow. That night I learned that my body is a true lightweight. Mrs. Whitman heard me getting sick and graciously came to check to make sure I was all right.

"Arden, are you okay?"

I saw this generous, graceful woman in her flannel and I panicked.

"You gave me food poisoning! Your food! Your cooking made me sick!!!!!"

I am pretty sure the purple wine mustache and stained lips gave away that I was lying. You don't really have a leg to stand on when your teeth are blue. With gracious compassion, the kind doctor looked down at me clutching her commode.

The next night, my tater tots were stolen from Willy's thieving fingers, the dog was humping my mother's ankle under the table, and Mary Hart was announcing celebrity birthdays on *Entertainment Tonight*. I'd never felt happier to be home.

Dollar, Dollar Store!

There ain't no shame in a day job, honey! Even if you have
artistic visions, a day job can be necessary. Everyone I know
in New York has a side hustle. And that doesn't mean that you
are not a success at your dream job—it just means that you
are SMART! Even my friend Tom, who was nominated for a
Pulitzer Prize for a play he wrote, kept his day job answering
phones at a law firm. Life is *expensive*, and when you walk into
a room to audition/pitch/interview *and* you have no cash in
the bank, it adds an extra layer of fear and panic.

I have a friend who was a series regular on a hit TV series
who kept her weekend waitressing job at a popular Italian
restaurant in Beverly Hills, through her second season on the
show because she knew how hard it was to land a good server
job at an LA restaurant.

No matter what kind of bonkers lessons you received from
your family, it is never too late to educate yourself about
money so you can become a BOSS BITCH. Growing up, I
got two very different lessons about earning a living. JJ was a
flat-out hustler. When she moved to Little Compton from the
big city to raise a family, she knew she wanted to be a baller
working lady.

Due to the size of Little Compton, the work options were
more limited than those in NYC. Because my mom didn't
think she would excel at being a lobsterman and she wasn't a

cop, she did the next logical thing: she got her real estate license and eventually opened her own real estate firm. That badass happily worked until the day she died. My mom loved working, and she hustled to provide for me and my brother. To this day I attribute my love of working from growing up with such an amazing role model.

The JJ side of my genes gave me the capacity to roll up my sleeves and get to work. I have had my own side hustles over the years. For instance, I was an elf at Macy's Santaland in NYC. My assignment was the photo elf, which meant that I was stuck inside Santa's tiny house with Santa, a man named Santa Phil. I am pretty sure Santa Phil was either narcoleptic or a drug addict. His skin always seemed to be very gray, and

he constantly had the sweats. He also had the pesky habit of frequently nodding off while the kids were on his lap. I was paid $7 an hour to wear a baggy elfin turtleneck and blowsy drop crotch elf pants and gently wake Santa Phil so people could "make their memories" with him. The only time Santa Phil would perk up was when a woman would come into Santa's house

Who's that naughty, sexy elf?

and flash her boobs at him. Suddenly Santa Phil was spry and on high alert.

"Ho! Ho! Ho! Who do we have herrrre?! I'm pretty sure somebody's on the naughty list!"

I also worked for my friend's dad, Mr. Stephens, doing data entry for sports marketing. It's a tricky thing working for one of your friend's parents because you find out quirks that you *realllllly* don't want to know about them. I quickly learned that Mr. Stephens was a total cheapo creeper. He would bring in holiday "bonus gifts" to the office for me and his assistant Kimberly. Nothing about his offerings actually resembled a present. For starters, they were unwrapped, and his "gifts" were always things like used pairs of his wife's old high heels, or a used Naugahyde business folder, or swag from various sporting events he had marketed that were clearly stained. The common denominator was that these items were not so minty fresh.

"Thanks, Mr. Stephens! I've always wanted a Sugarbush Mountain Ski 1998 beer koozie."

I'm pretty sure Mr. Stephens was decluttering his house and dumping the garbage spoils on his associates long before anyone in the world had heard of Marie Kondo and her "sparks of joy." I could deal with his clutter dump, but he lost me when he would say things to me like, "You have a cute face but chubby arms." That was my cue to get out of there. JJ supported my exit.

"You got places to go, kid! You don't need to be slowed down by an old jerk."

JJ was always about the hustle.

Willy, however, was more of a man of mystery. When he moved with my mom to Little Compton, he didn't appear to get another job for thirty years. Being out of the rat race of

New York City, it was like he suddenly decided to unofficially "retire" at the age of thirty. Although he was technically a CPA, he didn't seem to really work for anyone or go to an office. He did taxes for a few of our family friends, but other than that he was sort of a free agent. Aside from not earning any money, being out of the routine of going to work didn't do wonders for his self-esteem. One can get a little odd when no longer a part of daily functioning society. Growing up with both JJ and Willy really made me believe that work is good for the soul—it gives you dignity.

Willy seemed to perk up around the age of sixty and decided (for reasons unbeknownst to me) that it was time for him to reenter the working world—three months a year. He was on a mission and chose to get a job at a tax firm from January 1 through April 15 every tax season. In some ways, it was the happiest I ever saw him because he had structure, a place to go, and a job that made him feel useful. He was actually a really bright guy, so it seemed like it gave him some pride to be able to go into work.

Even in the midst of something as dry as accounting, Willy could apply his compulsive nature to it. He turned earning into a game, going so far as to invent his own holiday, which he dubbed Money Day. Despite his entering the workforce, my mother noticed that Willy still never seemed to have any cash. My mother discovered that Willy, a hoarder by nature, had saved up all his paychecks during his three-month gig working for The Man. One afternoon that lucky lady walked into her bedroom and discovered where all his paychecks had been going.

Rather than cashing his paycheck weekly, Willy had squirreled them all away in preparation for his big holiday—Money Day—when he cashed them all at once. That inspired visionary then spread the cash out on his bed like a little nest made out of money and cud, stripped down to his birthday suit, dove onto said cash pile, and proceeded to roll around in it.

His body was covered in twenties and nickels.

"What are you doing?!" my mother screamed.

"What does it look like I'm doing? Money Day!" he screamed back as he rolled around on his bounty, soaking up the magic of three whole months of hard work. Like a chubby man baby version of Demi Moore in *Indecent Proposal*, Willy was as happy as a pig in shit and was gleefully screaming, "Money Day! Money Day! Come on! Dive in!"

Grossed out, Janet was not in the mood to play Robert Redford.

"Put your pants on and remove the dollar from your ass before all of that money gives you hepatitis."

With that, Janet rolled her eyes and left the house to go back to her real job.

To celebrate Money Day, the rules were simple:

1. Save up all your paychecks until you really need the money.
2. Cash them all at once.
3. Spread out the cash on the surface of your choice.
4. Disrobe.
5. Get freaky with your Benjamins.

Even with the lure of Money Day, Willy's panic at having a job started earlier and earlier every year. The thought of work cutting into his matinees and hobby of aging Hostess products sent him reeling. Two weeks before his job began, Willy woke up early and did test runs with his Miata to make sure that he would make it to the office on time. (Yes, I said Miata.)

WOLF
MIC
xxxxxxxxx5030
3/11/2021

Item: ï¿½20010103875208 ((book)

My dad drove a candy apple red Mazda Miata convertible. It takes a strong man to drive a Miata. Willy liked to drive around shirtless with the top down, tanning himself to the color of a piece of beef jerky or a fancy lady's alligator clutch. Top down, oldies blaring, legally blind. Lucky, lucky, Rhode Island. Not only did Willy drive a Miata, this captain of industry had the confidence to get his own vanity plate.

This certified public accountant wanted people to know that he meant business when he pulled up for tax season. And what better way to let people know where you stand in your field than with a vanity plate. Willy's vanity plate read: CPA 2. He didn't want to get cocky—if you are not the number-one certified public accountant in Rhode Island, why brag that you are?

Say it loud, say it proud. Number 2 and LOVIN' IT!

The oddest part of Willy having a job was who he became when he was at work. This enigma had an alter ego when he was on the clock. Once Willy got to the office, he shook off his normally salty mood and was the King of the Charm Prom. The all-female accounting firm of Anders and Martin seemed to be some alternate reality he entered that chemically changed the entire makeup of his personality.

The first clue that worker bee Willy and "shut-in Boo Radley" Willy were polar opposites came when my mom and I ran into one of his coworkers at Chili's. Willy had tried to keep the ladies of the office from meeting us. We assumed he was having an affair, but we quickly realized he was hiding a much darker secret—Softy Office Willy.

"You're Willy's wife, aren't you?"

"Um . . . yeah? Can I help you?"

"I recognized you from the photo on his desk. You are so lucky to be married to Willy. He is such a teddy bear."

"Huh? Oh . . . funny, good one!"

But apparently these gals weren't joking. My dad had cast himself as the adorable confidant—think John Krasinski's or Bill Hader's character in a chick flick who all the ladies chat to about their problems.

"You deserve better, Rhonda. Tell him you won't move in with him unless you have a ring!"

"Way to stick with Weight Watchers, Dawn! You can't believe in anyone else until you believe in yourself!"

It was horrifying. Who was this guy? Crusty Willy I could trust; I was used to him, he was consistent in his behavior, but Sensitive Willy freaked me out. Thankfully, he reserved his charm exclusively for the ladies at the office. One morning, I was stunned to see my dad stomping out of the house laden not just with his normal man purse/cooler and bendy straws, but also dragging a gigantic teddy bear, a box of Russell Stover's chocolates, and a **CONGRATS ON THE BABY!** balloon in his stubby arms. Having never handled a balloon in his sixty-five years on the planet, the balloon seemed to be getting the best of him. As he was trying to shove a fistful of M&M's into his pockets for the daunting twenty-minute drive, he kept getting nailed in the head by the out-of-control helium-filled Mylar beast.

"How do I get this thing in my fucking car? Who invented this shit?"

"Are you about to go destroy a stranger's baby shower?"

"No. Kathy's finally pregnant. She and her husband have been trying for years."

"Wow! That's great!"

"I tried to tell her never to have kids, that they just suck you dry, but she didn't seem to listen. Neither did your mother."

At least he was consistent in his parenting advice.

And off CPA 2 sped in his Miata—a man baby and his gigantic balloon.

Come April 16 he was exhausted, and his alternate persona went back into hibernation. At which point he spent the next nine months resting up around the house and floating in the ocean to refuel for next tax season's work. Which is not to say that Willy had no work ethic at home. Give that man a household chore, and he would go to town on it like a person with OCD instructed to count all the tiles in Grand Central Station. He didn't F around when given a task. My dad had two chores in our house—the first was to empty the wastebaskets.

You always knew when it was 1 p.m. because you could hear Willy stomping around the house in his boxers screaming, "Goddammit! Why did you throw this sandwich away? It was perfectly good!"

Come 1:15 p.m. we were not allowed to use trash cans again for the rest of the day. Willy ran a tight ship! He was as punctual as Old Faithful and had the focus of a laser.

The fun always began after his main cleanup had been completed. My mom, my brother, and I loved to wait until the coast was clear, and then go from room to room placing one tissue in each newly emptied trash can.

"Goddammit. GodDAMMIT! Who put trash in the trash can!??"

And then he was off and running again.

It is important for a man to take care of his castle. Willy's number-one task in the house—aside from being freaky trash patrol and the official food ager—was to weed the patio. And weed he did. Slowly, methodically. One morning I stumbled out on the patio at the crack of noon. I was ready to treat myself to my favorite breakfast of champions, a jar of Skippy Super Chunk Peanut Butter and a spoon, when I noticed my dad seemed to be battling a killer weed with a very tiny tool.

"Shouldn't you use a shovel?"

"No—I'm fine! Is that my peanut butter?"

Rather than use a weed spray or a shovel, he was meticulously, with the focus of a serial killer, removing one stem at a time, wielding nothing more than a tiny, child's size Wild Bill Hickok souvenir pocket knife I had given him after a school trip to New Mexico. It was man versus weed.

"Are you sure you don't want a trowel or something?"

"I've got my system, smarty-ass," he said as he stuck a dirt-covered finger in my Skippy jar and scooped up a snack for himself.

Constantly dripping in sweat, he did all his weeding with no shirt or pants on. To do yard work clothed would defeat the whole purpose of tending to the patio—getting a tan. He didn't like to wear many clothes anyway, but while exerting any energy his bod needed to be free. He was like the hot construction worker in the Diet Coke commercials; only my dad was built like a seal, wore boxers, and wielded a penknife. It was weird when I brought friends over to the house. You never knew when an unclothed sixty-five-year-old day laborer was going to take a load off and want to chitchat, spread eagle in his boxer shorts, free-balling to make his new guests feel nice and comfy.

On he went all summer long, attacking his weed enemies brick by brick, inch by inch, with his novelty knife. He was so slow that by the time the whole patio was done, the first half that he'd weeded had grown back in. Willy would take it so personally when a weed grew back that he would mutter a string of expletives, tiny weeding knife in hand.

"Goddammit, son-of-a-bitch weed growing like it thinks it's the king of Weed Mountain."

Like Sisyphus forever pushing a boulder up a hill, Willy Myrin's patio would never, ever, ever, ever, EVER be weeded.

Bloom Bright, You Late Bloomer

No matter how invisible you feel in high school, you can always reinvent yourself in college or out in the world. It is never too late for a late bloomer! Blooming late just means you have to develop humanity, pathos, and a sense of humor, honey! I had no confidence or clue how to deal with guys until well into my thirties. My gut feeling is that you may actually have more admirers than you think you do. Let me tell you—I could NOT get dating right or even get laid in college . . . and I WASN'T EVEN A VIRGIN. But I tried! Oh, how I tried!

Before entering college, I had really gone that extra mile to ensure that I would lose my pesky virginity during my senior year of high school. I wanted to go off to college a sultry and sophisticated woman of the world. You'd think it would be easy—as a female—to lose your virginity, but that is not always the case.

I went to a small high school, which meant an even smaller pool of possible paramours. As senior year trudged on, it became clear that my deflowering was not going to happen of its own accord. Fall became winter, became spring, became prom, and still no action was happening in my pants. Finally, with graduation looming a mere six days away, I was a girl on a mission. Lose my virginity or bust! I had gotten a boyfriend the first week of May (just in the nick of time), and I was determined to graduate a full-fledged woman.

One disastrous evening on my quest to become deflowered, I had the horror of going on an awkward double date with our school's unofficial Varsity Sex Team. My new (indifferent) boyfriend, Sam, and I headed out for an evening with Eric and Pam, the couple in our class who humped seventeen times a day, like rabbits. I think every high school has that quiet couple who by all appearances are not the class horn dogs. Eric and Pam were a couple of good students, respected by the teachers, seemingly innocent, just two young kids in love. But the nasty truth was that they did it all day, every day, *everywhere*: school bathrooms, Pam's mom's car, basements, their neighbors' lawns, the woods, the biology classroom, Eric's dad's rowboat, behind the local gas station, in closets, and, yes, in Porta-Potties.

Off we all went for an evening of pool hopping and breaking into a public pool. Sam and I had not been dating very long, but sex was in the air! Not with me and Sam, but with Team Sex. To get into the pool, we had to scale a twelve-foot chain-link fence. Team Sex quickly scampered up and over the fence, stripped their clothes off, and were doing it like dolphins in the water within ten seconds of our arrival.

I was a little more hesitant. My clothes made climbing tough. When choosing my outfit for the night, I hadn't counted on the fact that our double date would consist of breaking and entering. To set the mood for seduction I was wearing my sexiest Annie Hall vest, bowler top hat, and an ankle-length circle skirt. Think fundamentalist Mormon meets Dora the Explorer—a look that is catnip to hot-blooded, eighteen-year-old males! That's right, I'm fashion forward! I took my closet of ready-to-wear knickers and went haute couture.

With great effort, I made it to the top of the fence—no easy feat in a floor-length skirt. So far, so good. Delighted that I'd made it to the top, it never dawned on me that getting *down* from the twelve-foot chain-link beast was going to be the *real* problem. I sat on top of the fence, stalling, trying to flirt with Sam before I had to jump.

"Wow, Sam—what a view! It takes quite a guy to plan such an exciting adventure."

"Hurry up. We're gonna get caught."

"I think I see the Big Dipper. Let's make a wish, Sam. 'Star light, star bright . . . '"

"Stop talking!"

I was distracted for a moment by the splishing, splashing, and slurping sounds coming from the pool. Team Sex was going for round eight for the day right in front of us. Awkward.

"Let's go! Ugh . . . do you need a hand?"

My increasingly grouchy companion was losing patience.

"No, thanks—just admiring the view. Wow, you really can see a lot from the top of a fence!"

"Whatever. Just jump down. Come on!!!"

"Not. A. Problemo."

I counted to three and decided just to go for it. I figured it would be good to execute an activity that would make losing my virginity seem like a walk in the park.

One, two, three . . . jump!

I closed my eyes, prayed for the best, and leapt. But the ground did not come. My lengthy circle skirt had gotten caught on the top of the fence and I was dangling by my waistband, ass hanging out for all to see, my body suspended ten feet in the air. The worst part was that I couldn't touch the ground, so I couldn't just lift myself off.

"Ugh!! Arden! What did you do!?"

Like it or not, Sir Douche-A-Lot was going to have to lend a hand. The predicament I was in felt worse than if I had landed and actually broken my femur.

More groaning came from the pool.

"I think I'm caught."

"Yeah. Clearly."

"Can you help me down?"

Sam sighed and removed me from the fence with great effort, while all along I had been hoping that he would remove my virginity. It was not to be. I did eventually lose my virginity that summer to my indifferent suitor. Was it spectacular? Not so much. We did it outdoors at a weekend-long party, and he left me in the same field in the morning. It also would have helped if he hadn't hooked up with my friend the next day.

When picking a boyfriend, consider dating someone who also wants to date you (and does not want to also hump your friends). That was a painful one. It took me many years to figure out how to pick better guys and better friends. Rule number one: Don't flirt with my friends, dudes! And with my girlfriends, my general rule of thumb now is: if your friend flirts with your paramour, byyyyyeeeeeee, Felicia! I didn't think I deserved better, and I picked both of them. I was certain that college was going to be a bigger, sexier man pond. Hot college men, here I come!!

When choosing a college, choose carefully and thoughtfully. Tour as many as you can, making a list of dream attributes.

Take your time and prudently weigh the pros and cons of each school—its size, academic focus, location, and so on. Then proceed to just go where your best friend goes, sight unseen, like I did. Perhaps "Don't think, just DO!" was not the best mantra for me.

I followed my best friend Sheryle to a small liberal arts college in Colorado. Being the product of not one but two hasty decisions (see: my parents' and my grandparents' engagements), I was not nervous in the least about my whimsical decision-making process. Look how my ancestors' impulsive decisions had turned out. I wouldn't be here if not for impulse control issues! Not to mention the fact that Sheryle had made a special trip to check out the college for us and had come home raving about all the hot guys on bicycles. She made this college sound like the school version of the Summer Olympics. Hot guys on bicycles? Sign me up!

My college was located in Colorado Springs, the witch capital (as in pointy hats and caldrons) and the 7-Eleven capital (as in tubular cheeseburger "rolls" cooked by a light bulb on a rotating roller grill display) of the United States. Colorado Springs at the time also boasted the third highest violent crime rate per capita in the United States. It had all the boredom of a small town mixed with the thrill of big-city violence.

While my college was a great school for many people, it was not the right fit for me. To be fair, I didn't have a ton of choices in schools, as I was not exactly rocking the honor roll in high school. Upon arrival at orientation, I got out of the car and was immediately filled with terror. I had never seen so many people adept at the hacky sack or so many different versions of white people with dreadlocks. Patchouli filled the air as boys named Turtle or Frosty wiled away the hours playing bongos in drum circles and wearing flowy man bloomers (not knickers, which would have been *marvelous*) while discussing mogul skiing and tripping their balls off on LSD.

The first guy I met in my dorm was Barry, a hefty bearded gentleman wearing a large maroon cloak who introduced himself as a "male witch." Bold call not to go with "warlock." He lived two doors down from me, had a wooden sword collection, and installed about fifty deadbolts on his door. I don't know if he was keeping us at bay or locking himself inside so he couldn't go after us. Either way, the effect was unnerving. Also, where the hell were the hot guys on bicycles? All I saw were lots of dudes who owned pet ferrets.

Apparently, a grave error had occurred. I had to get out of there. I made an appointment with the dean of the school and attempted to drop out the second day of orientation.

"Your Honor, I have made a big mistake. I accept that. But why should I be punished for my immature and foolish behavior for a year . . . and I'd like to get my money back." No go. The dean sent me to the school psychiatrist, who told me I was probably homesick. But I had never been more lucid in my life.

The second guy I met was a real go-getter, a guy named Chet who went by "Loft Guy" because he had bought a drill at Home Depot and set up a little business building lofts in dorm rooms. For fifty bucks, Loft Guy would build you a loft (or, as he billed it, a "two-story kingdom in your dorm room") out of rickety old plywood and rusty nails. Within the tiny twelve-by-twelve rooms, he created sleep platforms and storage for bikes, skis, and rock climbing equipment, complete with hammocks and housing for the numerous ferrets and iguanas that many students kept as pets.

Not to be outdone by Loft Guy, the student body as a whole spent a great deal of time working on their own crafting projects: perfecting the art of building the homemade bong. These male witches could build bongs out of apples, dolls, soda cans, old ski boots, lawn ornaments, trophies, water bottles, water guns, test tubes, paper towel tubes, Pringles cans, honey bears, pineapples, and even a Mr. Potato Head. If they had put the amount of time studying engineering that they put into bong construction, they probably could have built a space station on Mars.

Damn you, hot guys on bicycles who bewitched Sheryle! How the hell could I have been so careless? Damn you, Sheryle's libido! But I knew there was no one to blame but myself. I should have checked it out. *Obviously.*

Sheryle has always been less of a weirdo than I am and was quickly able to assimilate. She immediately found herself the only hot guy on a bicycle who actually bathed and was happily humping her way through freshman year. Taking my cue from her, I decided to try to make the best of it. This was college, after all; if I wasn't going to totally fit in, at least I could sexually explore my way to graduation!

Foiled again. It quickly became clear that not only did I not relate to these men in cloaks, these guys didn't have any interest in making out with the likes of me. Here are a few things that trust fund Rastafarian (aka Trustafarian) rock climbers who attended my school prized in a lady:

1. The ability to smoke large quantities of "kind bud" (aka medical-grade marijuana)
2. A never-ending supply of gorp (aka trail mix)
3. Sweet "bump skis" (aka skis for moguls)

4. A tight ass in Gore-Tex (aka a tight ass in anything)

5. Knowledge of the entirety of the Phish catalog

All the things I did not possess. I didn't stand a chance.

You want to talk about *Bachelor in Paradise*? I'm your girl. You want to smoke a bong and talk about mysticism? I'm afraid I'm out of my league. Not just because I don't know what mysticism is, but mostly because I can't smoke pot. Not for moral reasons. Pot hates me. I never met a brownie I did not like, until I ate three pot brownies.

Going to school in Colorado, you are forced to become at least passing acquaintances with marijuana. Most of the student body at my college seemed to have subscriptions to *High Times* magazine. To be fair, they were also all way more relaxed than me, laughing a lot and appearing to be having a much better time than I was. I figured they were on to something and decided to conduct my own drug research.

Never one for moderation, I dove right into the deep end of the pot pool. I found myself climbing one of Loft Guy's homemade lofts, nine feet in the air, to take a hit off "kind bud" from a ten-foot-long "super bong" constructed out of a soccer goalpost and duct tape. Not the brightest idea to go for a super bong when you are not sure how your body reacts to marijuana. (And you know, with certainty, that you are not exactly an expert in the drinking department.) As you can imagine, it was a total disaster, but I persevered. When you are in that kind of environment, you have to try to assimilate and attempt to become a stoner.

To make matters worse, I never smoked pot all by itself. Somehow it always seemed like a good idea to give pot a whirl after imbibing a couple of bottles of Boone's Farm Strawberry

Hill wine. It didn't occur to me that if you are experimenting with new vices, it is probably smart to try one at a time. Don't go for the "combo substance platter."

Never once did I get the giggles while smoking pot. I always went straight from "I don't feel anything" to "Why is everyone staring at me?" to "Oh fuck, I did it again. Everyone hates me. I am going to die."

When I smoke pot, not only do I become paranoid and paralyzed, I also stay that way for two to four days. Fun for all involved! All the stoners I knew were so jealous that I seemed to stay high forever, but none of them wanted to hang out with me and my creepy and intrusive stoner ways. I could ruin anyone's buzz.

"Hold my hand. For real, if you don't physically hold on to me, I will fall backward into the crack of the cushions of this couch. And get sucked into Middle Earth."

"If I don't concentrate on breathing, I will forget to inhale or exhale and I will die. And get sucked into Middle Earth."

Or the always popular move of running, giggling, down the hall only to bolt my door, hide under my rug (lest the boogeyman find me and take me away to Middle Earth), and vomit all night long into a bowl. Or some scenario like that.

When I surrendered and accepted the fact that I was at the wrong school, with the wrong group of people, with no prospects for sex and no capacity for drugs, I immediately fell into a massive funk. I grew super despondent, slept all the time, and gained thirty pounds. My room looked like a bomb had gone off in it. At one point, I lifted up my rug to find discarded pizza boxes, underwear, and sand. Not exactly the spoils of victory!

Normally fun and upbeat, the vampire in me completely won and I just slept all day, barely making it out of bed to go to my classes. My sleep issues hit rock bottom when I would snuggle attack people and make them nap with me. Usually this was fairly successful, as more often than not you could find some college student who has stayed out too late the night before and was more than happy to spoon away a hangover between classes. I was the nap pusher and hit a real low one afternoon when I forced my friend Lori to nap with me.

I woke up in a haze to find that Lori had vanished and in her place was a boy from our dorm—Ben Rabinowitz, or The Rabbi, as he called himself. The Rabbi was wide awake and watching me sleep. As much as I was in the market for male attention, waking up to a strange man watching you sleep is never a settling feeling for any female. I have never felt so creeped out in my life. I awoke to him smiling and saying, "You're dirty. You talk dirty."

In that moment, I knew that I had to pull myself up by the Janet Myrin bootstraps. I managed to escape, ran back to my room, and called home for moral support. My mom answered the phone and let me rant and rave about my own terrible decisions. After a few moments of silence, imitating my grandma, she said, "Arden, a card laid is a card played."

She was right. I had made my college bed, now I had to sleep in it. Or at least get out of it, make the bed, wash my hair, dust myself off, and generally get my shit back together. I had slept away most of my freshman year. But I could still get back in the game. No sex had occurred yet, but it wasn't a total bust. I had become a bit of a kissing bandit, making out with all sorts of hairy men who played the bongos. The best I did was make out with a guy who spent the night in my bed in my dorm room. In the morning, he and I woke up together.

"Hey, Eric, good morning."

"Morning, buddy."

With that, he hopped out of bed and ruffled my hair with what could be considered a slightly more affectionate version of a noogie. Then he threw on his outdoor wear and probably headed off to scale the side of a rock. I was done with Colorado.

My grades were in the toilet, but our school had an affordable arts program in Chicago. I didn't know much about it, but I applied anyway and they accepted me. I moved there my sophomore year and stumbled upon ImprovOlympic. It was amazing, and I felt like I had finally found my people. People who were funny indoor cats. I made sense here.

Creatively, I was inspired and awake and alive. Not to mention the added bonus that guys hit on me for the first time ever! I gained a little confidence and swagger. I also gained a few more pounds from the sexy combo of Sea Breezes and burritos. Turns out, guys in Chicago don't care if you look like a chubby Ron Weasley, because usually you are wearing a parka and they can't tell what your body looks like under all those layers anyway. A chubby wizard is fine with them. Oddly, there also seemed to be no women in Chicago. It was like the Alaska of cities! I was *el fuego*.

After a few months in Chicago, I was back to my old self. Filled with confidence after being pawed by extremely pale men in sweatshirts, I decided to go visit my girls Sheryle and Lori and do what I had not succeeded at doing up until that point—have a hot, drunken college hookup! I returned to Colorado for the last weekend of what would have been my sophomore year in a blaze of glory, having hitched a ride in a camouflage-painted Suburban with tinfoil all over the roof and antennas. My peers could tell I meant business. I still hadn't had sex in college, but I had the moxie and gumption to make it happen *that weekend*.

The first night back I went to a kegger and found the object of my affection. I laid eyes on this guy I had never met or even heard of, and he was hot as shit! Teddy Yonkers. He was a senior, he was cool, he wasn't wearing a cloak, he was graduating in two days, and he didn't know who I was. It was perfect.

I did what any college girl on the hunt for sex would do—I didn't talk to him or introduce myself. Instead, I ran back to Sheryle's dorm and made jokes about him for fourteen hours. I talked with the swagger and bravado of a longshoreman at fleet week. Oh, how I was obsessed with Teddy Yonkers.

"I am going to do The Yonks all night long!"

"The Yonks doesn't know what's coming his way, but one thing is for sure: Teddy Yonkers is going to get it—hard."

"Do you think the Yonks's mind is ready to be blown?!"

My much more sexually advanced friends humored me for a while until they finally couldn't listen to me anymore.

The next night was the final night of school, so the sex clock was ticking! I went to a blowout house party with Sheryle and Lori. All the usual suspects were there—the hairy but hot rock climbers, Chet the loft builder, the token naked guy (every school has one), Barry in his cloak, and some people tripping on peyote. The party was in full swing when I spotted my prey hanging out in the kitchen. Target locked on The Yonks. I sat in the corner staring and was mortified when my friends tried to make me go talk to him.

"Arden, he's graduating. You have nothing to lose; at least just go say hi."

I just watched him from afar and panicked when he caught me looking at him. He started to walk toward me, and I had to talk myself off the ledge.

Be cool, Arden. Act like a normal person. He doesn't know your weird operating system. You are a blank lady slate to him.

"Fun party."

"Oh, yeah. I always love Ben and Bill's house."

Fucking stupid. You can do better than that.

So I actually started talking to him. Like a normal person. I told him all about living in Chicago and improv. We talked about what he wanted to do when he graduated. We actually hit it off! We chatted for hours; I was flirty and coy and didn't act like a total weirdo. I was even able to play it casual, like I hadn't been calling myself the future ex–Mrs. Teddy Yonkers all afternoon. We were really clicking, and as the sun started to go down it felt like one of those magical movie nights. Not only was I maybe going to finally have sex in college, it might actually be with a really great, really cute guy with whom I clicked. As we left the party, we were chatting and walking toward his place. He was sweet and gentlemanly and hadn't even kissed me yet.

Finally, drunken college sex was going to happen! To me! I could sense it. And it was not even going to be creepy! When we got back to his house, Teddy kissed me. Sure, it was on his bong water–soaked futon, but I felt like I was Molly Ringwald in *Sixteen Candles* getting to kiss Jake Ryan. Falling into the eyes of this super-hot senior, I suddenly realized I had forgotten one pesky little detail.

Earlier that day, my friends were so sick of hearing me yam on and on about The Yonks that they decided to do something about it. As I was bragging and taunting about The Yonks, Lori's and Sheryle's sanity snapped. They grabbed two Sharpies, pinned me down, and drew all over my body. Written all over my torso, ass, and thighs were the words:

Do Me Yonks

A.M. + T.Y.

Mrs. Arden Yonkers!

I want Teddy Yonkers to touch me here (complete with arrows to my lady bits)

This crotch belongs to the Yonks! (more arrows to my crotch, softened by girlish hearts)

And that wasn't all of it—there were drawings of his penis, and each ass cheek had a drawing of a mustachioed villain on it.

This fine man, this hot stranger, had the possibility of removing the pants of a girl he had just met and finding on her thigh his name written in Sharpie on a drawing of a flaccid spaceship penis. *Holy shit!* And it was in Sharpie—I couldn't just wash it off. Those suckers were on my body for the long haul.

As Teddy's hand crept toward my blouse, I couldn't decide. What was worse? The possibility of being the only person in America to not have sex in college? Or him discovering that I had "Do Me Yonks" written above my crotch? Would I look like a creepy stalker who would keep someone under her floorboards? Even if I suggested that we turn out the lights, there was a possibility that our sweaty bodies would imprint—in mirror image—his name and penis cartoon all over his sheets.

I was really torn. Part of me was like "fuck it, let's do this!" I thought about playing it off like, "How did that happen?" Like it was a Criss Angel trick. "Oh, your name just appeared. How odd!"

I wanted it so bad! I wanted to scream, "Yonks, Yonks, do me, Yonks!" Instead, what popped out was, "I'm so sorry. I am really shy. Can we just spoon?"

Spoon?!! Are you fucking kidding me???!!!

If I had wanted to spoon, I could have gotten the Rabbi to hold me clothed and watch me sleep. Had I known I wasn't going to get laid junior or senior year either, I would have cut a hole in a sheet and told him I had a fetish for doing it dressed like a ghost.

Little did I know: my body is a vision board and it makes my dreams come true. Which is why I now always have *Do Me Idris Elba* written on my belly.

Don't Fuck the Drummer!

I see you, Sexy Drummer! I want you, Sexy Drummer! And for the love of God, I am going to run far, far away from you, Sexy Drummer!! For numerous reasons, many of us want to date the bad boy or girl. The dangerous one, the sexy mysterious one. The one who will hump you in an alley and give you chlamydia. There was no way I was going to grow up and naturally date nice guys after being raised by a father who would say zingers like "Look who's getting fat!" Needless to say, on my way to appreciating myself as the badass that I am, I made out with plenty of drummers. My "drummers" came in the form of aspiring actors, aspiring fashion designers, and aspiring comedians.

Okay, this will be a short chapter because, let's face it, *you're going to fuck the drummer.* I mean COME ON—he's the drummer! So maybe a better title for this chapter would be "So You Boned the Drummer—GOOD FOR YOU!" Get it, girlllll! (Or get it DONE, boy!) But at least *if* you fuck the drummer, you can execute it better than I did.

I was so paranoid about getting STDs that I was more of a make-out bandit. I never could relax and just sleep my way through my twenties with lots of people. It didn't help that when I was living in New York in my early twenties, I spent most of my time hanging out with my friends Sheryle and Katie (whom I had moved to the city with) and my brother,

Alarik, drinking Sea Breezes and watching *Party of Five* in my and Sheryle's basement apartment. I wanted to be wired like anyone other than me and just have fun and sexy one-night stands, so I grabbed the cup of condoms that JJ put on my dresser at the age of thirteen and said, "Let's take these for a spin!" Needless to say, I made some gentleman errors.

Sheryle and I becoming rapidly undateable in our basement apartment.

First, I made out with a guy named Flight Frenzy. I met Flight at a party, and he was sexy and cool and told me he was a professional glam rocker. Naturally I was intrigued since I mostly knew guys who were professional comedians or full-time fishermen. Glam rocker was a career option?! Let's see what this is all about! Flight asked me out on a date. The first half of the evening was fun—we went to his friend's recording studio. I tried to play it cool, like I always hung out with glam rockers in recording studios laying down sweet tracks.

When we met up, his pupils were the size of small pizzas, but who wanted their glam rockers sober? Not me! All my twenty-two-year-old brain could take in was the fact that he was so damn cute. And wearing a coat covered in feathers. The sex gods had brought me Flight and his Amazing Feather-Covered Dreamcoat!

After sitting for six hours watching him tune his guitar, he invited me back to his place, telling me that he wanted to "show me something." That sounded like it was either going to be really exciting or I was going to end up in a secret dungeon, but I rolled the dice and decided to go check it out. I figured he was a willowy glam rocker and he was losing muscle mass very quickly; if anything, this scrappy Rhode Island gal who grew up in a sea of boys could take him down.

Flight had a loft, which seemed fancy and exciting. On the one hand, his apartment was AMAZING. I mean, it was a full LOFT. I don't know where Flight got his money to pay for that loft. Maybe glam rocking was where all the Benjamins were hiding in New York? But I do know that what Flight had chosen to do with his loft was something I had never encountered before.

"I can't *wait* for you to see this, Garden!"

"It's Arden. Not Garden."

When we walked into his place, I saw that Flight had constructed a giant fake tree, complete with a treehouse, in the middle of his loft, and it was fully functional. We climbed up in the tree and as he shimmied around his man-made branches like a bejeweled spider monkey. I was wowed.

"Look at you go, Flight! You are agile! Scampering around!"

His treehouse was nicer than many of my friends' apartments. Most people I knew lived in alcove studios the size of a twin bed that they shared with one to eighteen roommates.

We giggled and made out, and it appeared my New York dream of hooking up with a hot musician was about to be complete. I was going to be a different type of woman who got it on with rock stars! Zayn Malik, here I come! All was going well . . . until we climbed down the tree to continue our evening. Flight hopped down from his perch and I followed, careful to slither down his tree in a sexier manner than when I had climbed that dreaded fence in high school. So far, so good; no circle skirts getting caught . . . and then BAM! I landed right in the middle of a pile of dog shit. *WTF?!* Surely this was a mistake.

I looked around and noticed there was not just one pile of indoor dog shit. His entire giant loft was covered in pile after pile of dog shit. How had I not smelled it? Where was this dog? I didn't see a dog anywhere. Was I that deluded by a cute face and the ability to play an instrument while wearing glitter eyeliner? What was even more alarming to me was the fact that Flight didn't seem bothered by it, embarrassed, or in any hurry to clean it up. How could you invite a lady over for a date and not scoop up all the fecal matter that was all over your floor?

As much as I wanted to be the cool girl hooking up with a rock star, where the fuck was his dog?? Even a cute face could not make up for the fact that his floor was covered in (hopefully) dog shit. I panicked, came up with some lame reason why I had to get out of there, and RAN.

Nevertheless, I was still young and on the prowl in New York, and I felt like I needed to get some notches on my bedpost. I got the opportunity one magical spring night when I got invited to go to the season finale party of *Saturday Night Live* that they hold every year on the ice rink. It was a dream come true— the whole cast and guest host stay out till the sun comes up. I put on a vintage velvet coat that had black feathers all over it (Flight inspired the glam flapper rocker inside me), headed

down to 30 Rock and into the party. My childhood dreams felt
so close. That night I was at the epicenter of comedy, living in
Manhattan, near the Rainbow Room, admitted to *SNL* for one
evening. I got the Golden Ticket for the night. So close, yet so far.

I danced all night and met the cutest guy, Jared, who had
a show on MTV that he was doing with his friends out of the
back of a van. Jared was sweet and adorable. He looked like a
surfer and seemed to be funny and nice. We made out on the
dance floor, and after my disastrous non-hookup with Flight, I
decided that this was my chance. I invited him back to my place.
We hopped in a cab as the sun was coming up and made our
way back to my apartment. I felt like Holly Golightly as we sped
past Tiffany's in my vintage outfit with the sun coming up and
this cute guy by my side.

Jared and I were tired and tipsy, but we made out and
climbed into my bed, and I actually was able to relax enough
that I was ready to fuck the drummer! Okay, maybe not "the
drummer," but "the guy in the van." I guess that doesn't sound
quite as cool. Nevertheless, we had fun and passed out, and I
woke up in the early afternoon to the cutest boy in my bed and
my phone ringing. (This was back in the day when people still
had land lines and answering machines.) My brother was calling
from a payphone.

"Arden. It's me. I'm on the corner. I need to come over."

"Who's that?"

"Oh, that's just my brother. Ignore him."

The phone rang again. And again. And again. Alarik left
message after message. My brother had never *ever* been in such a
panic to talk to me.

"Hello? PICK UP! I know you're there."

"Yo, dude! It's me. PICK UP! I need to come over. I need to use your bathroom. BIG TIME."

"Just ignore him."

I love my brother, but I wasn't going to let him cock block me the one time I was able to let loose and have a really fun one-night stand (which could turn into more?). This was the cutest boy that had been in my bed in YEARS. I couldn't deal with my brother ruining this for me. I looked over at what I had ensnared in my bed and gave him a kiss and we started making out. Things were looking up for your girl here! Until . . . my buzzer started ringing on my apartment. Alarik had SHOWED UP.

"I know you are here! LET ME IN!!"

WTF!!!????? How could this be happening to me!!?? And from my *brother* of all people? Let me make it clear: one of the things I learned growing up in the Myrin household is that you never drop in on anyone unannounced *ever*. You *never ever* just drop by. It's not cool; people need warning.

"Maybe you should let your brother in? It sounds like he really wants to see you."

NO. FUCKING. WAY. NOT TODAY, DEVIL!

"Nah, I see him all the time. Just be quiet, he'll go away."

And then the unimaginable happened. I saw two hands on the bars outside my window.

At the time, I was living with Sheryle in a rent-controlled duplex apartment. We had the basement and the ground floor. My bedroom faced the street and was about twelve feet up above street level. It may have only been twelve feet off the ground, but in order to see in my bedroom it was still a bit of a hike.

My brother was scaling the outside of my apartment building like Spiderman and hoisted himself up, pushing his face through the window and catching me in bed with my very first one-night stand. Why did the gods want to foil me??? DAMN YOU, SEX GODS!!!! Begrudgingly, I let Alarik in.

Jared gathered his clothes and quickly scurried out of there.

"What the fuck, Al??? You just cock blocked me!!"

"Move it!"

Alarik raced past me to the bathroom.

"Sorry, dude. I was trying to impress a girl and seem like I was a social activist, so I volunteered for the AIDS walk in the park."

"Was she impressed?"

"Yeah, until I got diarrhea and there are no public restrooms. So I came over here."

It was pretty obvious that both Myrin children needed to work on their seduction games if we ever hoped to successfully navigate getting laid in Manhattan. To be fair, as most of our ancestors married on a dare, we weren't the most versed in the mating arts.

Don't Date the Drummer!

Okay, so you fucked the drummer. I get it. But now you want to *date the drummer*?! Ooooh, honey, it's harder to date the drummer than it is to fuck the drummer. Think of the drummer like a rare hothouse flower that needs to be free!!!!! Dating the drummer may lead to one or more of the following: the drummer fucking your friends; you covering the drummer's rent; the drummer stealing all your Adderall; the magical world of ghosting; you inviting your friends to one of the drummer's gigs and finding out that the drummer is not as talented as you thought he was (that's a real lady-boner killer). (Unless that drummer is Josh Dun. And you are Debby Ryan. In which case, you can and SHOULD marry the drummer! Because he is the BEST DRUMMER.)

I wish I could time travel to my little twenty-two-year-old self and tell her, "Don't date potential, girl!!" It's always a warning sign when you think, *He would be so great if he didn't yell at his mom in front of me.* (Peeps—if your paramour yells at their mom in front of you, just know, at some point they *will* yell at you.) I should have run when the first time I met my boyfriend's mom was when I walked into a room and he was screaming at her.

"Dammit, Shelley!!!! I told you not to bleach my jeans!"

He was twenty-five, didn't do his own laundry (or pay rent), and used to say things to me like, "Well, if all else fails, you can just be on a sitcom."

I was on a sitcom. And I had worked my ass off to get there. Now mind you, I didn't know he was a career-belittling mom yeller when I first met him. I just saw a sexy bad boy clothing designer. I should have just slept with him and then moved on. Or better yet . . . RUN in the first place.

Unlike buying a fixer upper in real estate, I am a true believer that *dating* a fixer upper is a dangerous game. When you think to yourself any of the following—*I'm the only one who really "gets" him. He just needs someone to see his true potential. If only he could just focus and get that massage license*—no, honey. Let someone else clean up that mess. People are not like houses. You can't just throw shiplap, a sliding barn door, and a NAMASTE sign on someone and make them a keeper.

My road map was obviously off. I only knew what a relationship looked like from two people marrying on a dare. The people in my family all skipped the dating part and went right from one round of cocktails to meet you at the altar! Dating was uncharted territory for me. Add to that the fact that for many years I clearly had a broken picker. You show me the worst man in the room—sign me up!

I dated a lot of not-so-great guys. I didn't think I deserved better. My dad would always say, "I feel sorry for anyone who wants to marry you." Pretty awful thing to say to your daughter. That stuff trickles down. I am here to tell you: if you grew up with people telling you not-so-nice things about you—no matter what—you are lovable. You are valuable. You do have worth. You deserve some fox who lets you do your thing (and also doesn't yell at their mom).

The most common denominator I had was picking guys who eventually slept with my friends. Not only did my "friend" sleep with my boyfriend the day after I lost my virginity to him (remember Sam?), but over the years, and on more than one occasion, once I was interested in or started dating a guy, my friends would then start hitting on him. It was like my interest in a guy was catnip for the women I hung out with. I had to really do some soul-searching and cull the friend and love-interest herd.

I needed to do things differently. I didn't know how to reconcile the silly, sparkly gal that people would meet at a party with who my dad told me I was (and who I feared may have been secretly correct). Moving to LA for a job and being 3,000 miles away from Willy gave me a chance to see that maybe I wasn't so bad, that maybe who I had been told I was was wildly off base. I worked really hard at separating what I had been labeled as with who I really was. Slowly and surely, I began to like myself. I started picking nice friends who supported me (and did not use my love interests as their Tinder). I was performing and writing. I was actually setting up a big, happy life.

I started to date nicer guys and go slow and steady. I had to remember that not every guy was out to get me, and to give them the dignity of their own experience. I also stopped "trauma bonding" with guys. By that I mean meeting a guy and bonding over being hurt in a past relationship, or a tricky parent or whatever. I figured I should give someone I was starting to date (and me) the chance at seeing if we had real potential without all of our ghosts in the room.

I would go to movies and museum exhibits and take interesting classes just to have something to talk about beyond the fact that I felt like perhaps something was horribly wrong with me. I do believe water seeks its own level, and the more I shined myself up from the inside, the brighter my light shone, attracting nicer people. Which is not to say I knew what to do with them once they arrived.

You have more than one guy taken away from you and it makes you a little territorial. In general, I am a pretty low-key girlfriend, but I am not too proud to say that even when I did start dating nice guys, I still had the capacity to behave like a first-class d-bag.

One night, a few weeks into dating a great, very hunky guy named Dan, he and I decided to go to our first party together. No big deal. What could go wrong? I was proud to show off the fact that I could attract (and not run from) a guy who wouldn't steal things from the host's medicine cabinet and wore shirts with real buttons! I had never dated a guy who actually *wanted* a girlfriend before, so it was odd to be with someone who was emotionally available. (And his apartment was not covered in shit!)

Dan was handsome and nice and seemed to like me, and that immediately made me highly suspicious. He had also been in the Air Force, which is something I had never had contact with. We Myrins don't have a huge sense of civic duty. Remember, I come from a long line of draft dodgers and gentlemen farmers. Dan was so cute and sweet that I knew there had to be a catch. He also never wore shorts, and one day when he scratched his leg his pants lifted up and his leg looked a little smooth and waxen. Holy shit! I became convinced that Dan had a wooden leg.

I called Alarik to run it by him.

"If I was dating an amputee, would that be weird?"

"Why? Are you getting kinky?"

"No—I think this guy I just started to see may have a wooden leg."

I made up a whole backstory in my brain—how at some point during his time in the Air Force he must have been in heavy combat and lost his leg as service to his country. (I later learned his service included no combat, and mostly consisted of painting the higher-ups' houses at his base in Louisiana.) Turns out I am totally out of my mind, and Dan had both of his limbs; he just hated shorts.[13]

I had done the work on myself to start attracting nicer guys, but that didn't mean I had any idea how well-adjusted people dated—I just knew how to hang out with comedy guys, make out with someone, or get married on a dare. I was completely out of my comfort zone starting to date Dan. For a while I exhausted myself attempting to appear "normal."

It started with trying to clean my tiny house. (Until the age of thirty-five I'd never lived in a dwelling larger than five hundred square feet.) I would hide all my belongings and make an effort to seem tidy and be like an early riser. When Dan came over to my place for the first time, I thought I had hidden all my piles and went out of my way to make it tip-top clean.

"Wow! Great place! I love how messy you are!"

WTF?!!! "What are you talking about? I'm not messy."

"Yes, you are—you're a mess and I love it."

This fucker was freaking me out.

Off we went to a party with his single buddy Toby. Once we got there, a gaggle of girls descended upon Dan and Toby. One lady in particular—let's call her Cruella de Vil—really hit it off with Dan, and they sat and chatted the night away, giggling and talking.

---

13. If you are interested in learning more about Dan Martin's funny adventures in the Air Force, I highly recommend his hilarious book of essays about it called *Operation Cure Boredom*.

I headed off to the bar to calm my nerves with a few Sea Breezes and watched them having the time of their lives, giggling, laughing. I got more and more buzzed from the sidelines and started complaining to a friend, Erinn, about the ho-bag who was hitting on my man. I decided it was time for me to change my pattern of letting other women take my guy, and I wasn't going to just roll over and play dead; I was going to summon up my inner "Real Housewife of New Jersey" and fight for my man!

I steeled myself, approached Dan, and whispered, "How's it going? What are you doing?"

"Oh, I am just chatting with Cruella here—trying to hook her up with Toby."

Uh-huh. I have two eyes and can tell you Cruella didn't want Toby; she wanted Dan.

But I didn't want Dan to know how crazy I was, so I decided to play it cool.

"Well, I'm super busy, too. When you get bored playing matchmaker you can come hang out with me where the fun people are."

Note to self: if you are trying to seem mysterious and alluring, never refer to where you are hanging out as "where the fun people are."

I made a beeline to the bar.

"A Sea Breeze for me and one for my 'friend' here."

My friend was my left hand.

I double fisted my lame lady cocktails and watched Dan and Cruella like a government spy stalking a sleeper cell. Hand touch, laughter, whispers. *NOOOOOOOO!!!!!!!!*

I dragged Erinn outside and decided I needed to take up smoking. Bumming one from a barfly, I set out to calm my nerves.

"That skanky ho is all over him! Putting her stank on him!!"

That "skanky ho" also happened to be beautiful, elegantly dressed, and very successful. A woman's nightmare trifecta of qualities locked and loaded on my man.

I, on the other hand, was twenty-eight and wearing pigtails like Chrissy from *Three's Company* and had on a T-shirt that read: ARDEN—I LIKE TO PARTY!

I started pacing back and forth across the bar, glaring at them. My expression was the closest approximation to an angry snake that I could come up with—slits for eyes, lips pursed up to my nose, glare locked on my target.

Back and forth I paced like a caged puma.

At one point, I did a nice little drive-by of the happy couple and whispered in Dan's ear, "I will fucking kill you."

Crisp. To the point. Riddled with self-esteem.

My hot gin breath, heavy on his neck. I had to reach up on my tippy toes to whisper, as the genetically superior couple stood a full head taller than me.

Much to my horror, Dan just looked down at me, totally puzzled. "Um . . . okay."

And he *kept talking*. (I'm not saying that just because I "worked on myself" that there wasn't a learning curve on implementing what I'd learned. This was new territory for me, my bunnies!)

I have never seen a guy more elaborately trying to hook his friend up. Cruella was totally into him. And who could blame her? Dan was a babe, he was a war hero, and he was nice. But more important, he was MINE!!!!!! I needed a nice guy!!!! My rage grew with the beating of a drum inside my head.

Again, I retreated to the other side of the bar and sulked to Erinn.

"It's going to happen again. I am watching as my guy is taken by another girl—right in front of me. Again!"

I felt crazy. Erinn took me outside and ran me in little laps like a golden retriever on the sidewalk to calm me down.

"Here's what you are going to do. Stop being such a total weirdo. Just go join the conversation, Arden. You don't have to hide from him. He's with you."

"You're right. I'm going to join in and remind him of the fine piece of tail he has waiting for him."

Classy.

Emboldened by our conversation, I tightened my pigtails and stumbled off across the bar. My five Sea Breezes and two Marlboro lights were starting to kick in, but I figured that would just make me seem loose and fun. Note to self: three Sea Breezes and one Marlboro Light is the *maximum* amount you can ingest to seem loose and fun. After that point, Arden, you just seem like a loose cannon.

I joined in and glared up at the two of them.

"Hello, you two!"

"Umm . . . hello?"

"Arden, this is Cruella."

"Uh-huh . . . "

Time stood still as I decided how to properly proceed and let Cruella know that Dan had his hands full with a classy, elegant catch of a lady. What happened next was not what I had set out to do, but truly is the basis of my wiring. I decided to take matters into my own hands. Doormat no more!!!

I knew from "working on myself" that when setting a boundary, it is best to mindfully choose your words and actions to represent who you are as a person. Before I knew it, I found myself crouching over and rubbing my ass up and down the thigh of my date. Aggressively up and down, all the while making creepy eye lock with Cruella and grinning a victor's grin.

"Arden, what are you doing?"

"Cruella knows what I'm doing . . . I'm spraying my turf!!!!!"

Arden: 1. Cruella: 0.

SCOREBOARD, BABY!

Rub, rub, glare, glare.

"I'm just spraying my turf with my inky spray," I muttered as I pointed a finger right at her face and then sauntered away, assuming my job was done.

And it was—I married that guy. Who could blame him? Inky spray really has a "put a ring on it" quality to it. (And he didn't even have to dare me.)

Me and my Rock of Dan-braltar.

The Unofficial Grand Chancellor of Personal Safety

It is important to take risks in life. Without a little chutzpah, you can just end up living in your parents' basement, binge watching *Queer Eye*, while gearing up to attempt to make eye contact with the UPS guy. *However*, there is a big difference between taking healthy risks and being needlessly reckless. I have always considered myself the Unofficial Grand Chancellor of Personal Safety. While I may be an adult woman who broke her vagina doing the Worm and burned her eyeball with a curling iron, I am very careful with myself in any activity that is blatantly life-threatening.

The summer after fifth grade, at the age of ten, I begged to be sent to sleep-away camp. All my friends had signed up for a camp in Vermont, and my little brain became locked and loaded on figuring out a way to get JJ to agree to let me go. I wanted a month of freedom in the woods, making lanyards, hearing ghost stories, and singing "Kumbaya" by the campfire. And come on! Who didn't want to go away to summer camp after seeing *Meatballs* or *Little Darlings*?[14] If it was good enough for Bill Murray and Kristy McNichol,[15] it's good enough for me!

---

14. Both are classic sleep-away camp movies.
15. Kids, millennials, national treasures: Kristy McNichol was an early '80s teen star of *Little Darlings* and the *foxiest tomboy* in all the land, who had smokin' feathered hair and got to make out with a young, hunky Matt Dillon.

"It would be really good for me, Mom. I can practice my independence and learn how to take care of us if the world comes to an end and we all have to live in the woods."

"I'm not living in some yurt that you built."

I begged and pleaded. Not only did we not have the money, but it was impractical—we lived in a town where the main industry was summer tourism. The magic of being a full-time resident of Little Compton meant that for three months a year, our normally sleepy town was hopping. Hopping if you like clambakes, boogie boarding, and hitting mailboxes with baseball bats. People come from far and wide to spend their summers in Little Compton, but I craved adventure and independence. I wanted to socialize in the woods! I made charts explaining how it is good for a child to spend time in the great outdoors and a list of famous people who loved camp.

"How else am I supposed to be the next Davey Crocket, Franklin Delano Roosevelt, or flame-haired blues singer Bonnie Raitt?"

It was a stretch financially for my parents, but my mom finally relented and saved up money where she could.

"Who needs a new roof?" she asked me sarcastically.

I had to agree as I didn't think buying a new roof seemed like a fun way to spend cash.

I was so excited. I loved the idea of summer camp—the late nights, playing Bloody Mary and Light as a Feather–Stiff as a Board, the smell of pine trees, and dances with guys from the neighboring boy camps. I got my paws on a hand-me-down steamer trunk and started getting myself ready for my big going-away experience. I packed my best tube socks, T-shirts with iron-on rainbows, my brother's old alligator shirts, my sportiest knickers, bug spray, and my grandpa's old canteen covered in fake fur. I was *ready*!!

Off I went to the woods of Vermont to Camp Farwell, the first girls' summer camp established in the United States. My friends and I all preordered the T-shirts: CAMP FARWELL—A PLACE FOR GIRLS TO SHINE! above a logo of a horse whose mane was blowing in the wind. That should have tipped me off to a major fact right there: all my friends who were going to Farwell were "horsey girls"—those gals in class who carried plastic horses in their lunch pails.

At our cafeteria table, they would pull their tiny horses out and make "jumps" and riding courses out of their milk cartons and old Doritos bags. Making whinnying sound effects, they galloped their plastic friends through an edible arena as I stuffed my face with my Fluffernutter sandwich and guarded my food.

"This is Greased Lighting! He's a two-year-old shy stallion who loves dressage almost as much as he loves carrots!"

When I arrived at Camp Farwell, it was beautiful—a quintessential New England camp, with pine cones scattered everywhere on a picturesque little lake complete with a flotilla, slide, and canoes. There were loads of cabins and a big, gorgeous barn. I was bursting with excitement *until* a few girls whinnied up to the car all wearing classic equestrian jodhpurs and velvet riding hats, cropping each other with tiny whips.

"Welcome! What cabin are you in? I hope you're in Talk Derby to Me!"

Shit. I had willfully blinded myself to the fact that I had begged my mom to enroll me in a "horse camp." There was one small glitch—I hate horses. Not the animals themselves—they are stately, attractive creatures. Rather, I hate *riding* horses.

I have personal safety issues and value my life. As such, I have a healthy respect for anything that is way larger than me, alive, and has teeth and a mind of its own. You do your thing, I'll do mine, animal kingdom! Why throw a saddle on a large animal and try to ride it? Seals are bigger than me, too, but I don't try to ride them. Because I like myself. (And the texture of seals seems creepy.) To me, a good rule of thumb is: if something is not made out of metal, don't use it as your mode of transportation.

I had ridden a horse exactly *one time*. That was enough for me. My friend Cindy had a birthday party at one of the local farms, and there were pony rides. While all the other girls were having the time of their lives, I just wanted my pony to walk in a circle on a tether. Carefully. When it would trot or bend its head down, I freaked out.

"He's eating grass! He's eating grass!"

I thought my response was perfectly reasonable, *because a horse is alive and 1,200 pounds heavier than me.* Cindy and my friends just waved at me as they cantered by. I couldn't believe I had unwittingly begged and pleaded to sign up for a month at a camp where the main activity was my own personal Tower of Terror.

Turns out the horses themselves were the least of my problems. What was a much scarier component of horse camp was the company I was forced to keep—150 horsey girls surrounding me in the woods. I never fully took into account just how creepy it would be spending a month among girls who were weirdly obsessed with their horses.

Look, I have obsessions myself. I get it. I love *The Bachelor*, makeup pallets, and karaoke. Even at a young age I had enjoyed my fair share of crushes. But my crushes were on humans, not on horses. I would have made out with River Phoenix or Kirk Cameron[16] in a heartbeat. Not so for these young gals; these tiny tots were pining away for their horses. Scratched all over their diaries were doodles like:

Lauren + Lighting Bolt! True Love 4 Eva!!
Stacey loves Butterball!!!
Mrs. Rachel Abracadabra-Silverman

Rather than playing Truth or Dare, my bunkmates would set up jumps in our cabin and trot around. They wanted to brush and braid my hair and give me a horse name.

"We're going to call you Leon Trotsky."

I am proud to say that for the entire month, I did not once set foot in the barn of my own accord. Janet did not raise a drip, so I rolled up my sleeves and decided to make the best of it. I signed up for every other activity that the camp offered to avoid the barn. Often, I was the only person in archery, pottery, or canoeing.

I have never been sportier or more of a "joiner" in my life. I even got to star in the all-girl production of *Oliver Twist*—the first of many men's roles I was to play before I developed boobs. The Artful Dodger was a natural fit for me, what with my love of knickers and my jaunty young man's haircut. All they needed to do was put me in a ratty old top hat, some fingerless gloves, and smudge my face with charcoal, and I was ready to be a young male pickpocket scamp!

As the summer wore on, the girls' love affairs with their horses intensified. There were gymkhana shows, and the girls

---

16. This was before he explained how evolution works while peeling a banana. LOOK IT UP!!!!

were feeling protective and competitive of who would get to ride what horse at the big event. They needed the right horse to proudly show off their riding skills.

"Mr. Wizard really seems to feel more at ease when I am riding him. Sorry, Shannon. We just have more of a connection."

It felt like the crazier the horse was, the more the girls wanted to ride him.

"No one understands Wind Dancer like I do; sure, he's a biter, but he's misunderstood. He doesn't mean it when he bucks."

Girls are truly messed up if they even prefer a bad boy *horse* to a nice one. I have never seen a more sexed-up group of girls. They would ride each other around on all fours, going from the cabins to the canteen, occasionally binding each other in little homemade harnesses. God forbid the girl being "ridden" start to whinny or buck; she would promptly have her ass whipped with a crop, as she "needed to be broken." *Fifty Shades of Horsey*.

There were a few cabins full of gorgeous and filthy rich girls from New York City and Greenwich, Connecticut. It seemed unfair that they should all be so rich *and* so gorgeous. It was only later in life that I realized their banker dads had married trophy wives (Swedish stewardesses, et cetera) and thereby elevated the visual gene pool.

While externally the girls looked very put together and cute, this was a group of jodhpur-wearing deviant weirdos. We kept having all-camp meetings because someone took a shit in the shower. (The head of camp actually called it a "B.M.," and it took me a few days to find out that B.M. was the elegant way of saying bowel movement, aka gigantic shower shit.) These little blond girls were sick fucks.

As the summer wore on, the girls got more and more insistent that I needed to give horses another chance. They staged a horse intervention on me in my cabin, All This 'N Heaven Too (I guess even horsey girls can't resist a name sounding like an '80s movie), a cabin full of ten-year-old girls on the mid-to-low level of the popularity scale.

"We've all been talking about it, and as a cabin we feel like you really need to give the horse community another chance."

"We just want to show you the horses as we see the horses— as the most magnificent and glorious creatures on the planet."

Didn't they know that horses could shake you off and trample you in a heartbeat? Did no one realize they were *alive*???!!

"I'm good. But thanks. I'm really loving learning how to sharpen a knife with a rock in the wild."

"We're not taking no for an answer."

When someone says, "We're not taking no for an answer," that is your cue to run screaming for the hills. With that, the girls of All This 'N Heaven dragged me, kicking and screaming, up to the barn, where I was handed carrots and sugar cubes to feed to their horse boyfriends.

"Are you sure he's not going to bite my hand off?"

"Yes. See, it's easy; they love it. Just bend your fingers back like this and hold your palm out. You wuv it, don't you, don't you, Captain Sprat?"

I had never seen anyone baby talk to an animal before, and I was pretty sure I never wanted to see it again. To appease my captors and get the hell out of the barn, I relented. I took a deep breath, closed my eyes, and held my hand out with a few sugar cubes on it for the good Captain Sprat to eat.

A moment later all I could feel was teeth, snot, and a sandpaper tongue the size of a dessert plate all over my hand.

"He likes you!"

Captain Sprat snorted and sprayed me with stringy drool and horse snot.

"Ew! That is nasty!"

"It's just horse spit. He's just saying hello."

I was out of there.

I needed to appeal to JJ to come rescue me from my horse captors. When pleading your case, make it clear right out of the gate that you are not a sissy. I would send carefully crafted letters home:

Dear Mom,

I am not homesick. However, no matter how much I beg and plead you, I am writing to tell you do not, under any circumstance, give into my demands and send me back here next year. Even if I am driven tearfully to my knees, do not listen to my pleas. Also, if you miss me and need me to come home now, I would not fight that. You can find me at the archery practice range.

Love,
Arden

No go. JJ was less than thrilled reading my letters under her leaky roof.

When the summer ended, my fellow campers were weeping and clutching the necks of their horses in the barn, as if they were all Romeo and Juliet being torn apart. Except Romeo was a horse.

The last night of camp we all sang "Leaving on a Jet Plane," and I put on the performance of my life. I wept and wept and made promises to see my new best friends next year at camp. It is the one and only time of my life I have been able to cry on cue.

Once I got home, I vowed that I would make it my mission to make smart safety choices in life—which is the moment I vowed to become the Unofficial Grand Chancellor of Personal Safety! In high school, I would ride my bicycle to a keg party so I wouldn't have to drink and drive home. I could deal with a few scratches from bushes if I swerved into them. Thankfully, I lack any athletic skill whatsoever, so sports-related injuries were out. I sailed through high school with all my limbs intact. And then I got to college.

I did not count on the fact that college, though billed as an institution of higher learning, is in reality the epicenter of stupidity. One of the things about college that is so alarming is being in close proximity to so many people who seem to have no regard for their personal safety. In addition to making out with hockey players who clearly had open sores on their mouths, the college gals seemed happy to go along with whatever outings were being dreamed up by hormonal teenage guys.

My freshman year in college, I went on a real live spring break. Sheryle talked me into hitting the road for a thirty-person road trip. Off we caravanned to Arizona to spend a week at Lake Powell: home to party boats, booze cruises, and sunburned drunk white people. It was my biggest nightmare: being drunk on the open waters under the blazing sun—a deadly combo for a lightweight natural redhead like me.

I thought my biggest enemy would be the piercing desert sun and the jungle juice that we were all drinking. Wrong. I didn't count on the reckless activities that take place when eighteen-year-old dudes are in charge of the party itinerary. When we weren't drunk swimming, drunk boating, or drag racing against other drunk boaters, we spent our time cliff diving into the world's largest man-made lake. I knew cliff diving was a terrible idea from the moment we drove our party barge to the jumping spot—a cliff that appeared to be eighty feet high.

The Unofficial Grand Chancellor of Personal Safety was on high alert! Who knew how deep the water was, or if there were rocks underneath. You can't tell just by *looking* at a (man-made) lake how deep it is. Maybe the people who built the lake got tired of digging that day. Had anyone gone underwater and measured it or done a sweep of the water for rocks? I think not!

What if a party boat had sunk there and was still lurking a few feet underwater waiting for someone to get speared on its mast when they belly-flopped off the cliff? The whole thing seemed like a terrible idea. I was going to suggest that we turn around when suddenly everyone started cheering as the guys raced off to the top of the cliff. This was like the opening scene in a teen horror movie.

Off they went, one after the other, flinging themselves gleefully off the cliff. Jackknifing and diving, everyone was high-fiving and having a blast. I decided to rally the ladies on the boat.

"This is a bad idea, right, ladies?"

Silence. Much to my horror, I was soon alone on the boat. Sheryle and all the other young women decided to take in the fun and had raced off to join the jumpers. Sheryle, Lori, Carrie—off they all went. Squealing and laughing, the gals had embraced cliff diving.

Pretty soon I was the last female standing. My friends had betrayed me.

"Arrrrdeeeennnnnn!!!!! Do it!!!"

"No thanks."

"Do it!!! Do it!!! Do it!!!! It's fun!"

"I'm good."

It was like a hacky script in an after-school special about peer pressure. The sad thing about peer pressure is it works on me. Eventually I was so sick of people pestering me that I begrudgingly relented.

"Fine. I'll jump once—okay?"

I climbed up to join all the revelers and looked down. It suddenly seemed a thousand feet high. I like roller coasters, but this was insane.

"One . . . two . . . three . . . jump!!"

I jumped. I did not dive. I was soaring and flailing through the air feet first. Before I knew it, I was rocketing into the water. I was safe. Sort of. My entry into the lake felt like what can best be described as an enema the size of Lake Powell rushing up my asshole. I had just lost my anal virginity—to a man-made lake.

"Yeah, Arden! Woo-hoo!! Wasn't that fun?"

"It was something."

"Yeah!"

People were swimming up to high-five me. I was surprised there was any water left for anyone else to swim in, as surely all of it had moved into my lower body cavity. And then it got worse. What goes up must come down. Oh no. *Oh nooooooo.*

We were all out on the lake, all thirty of us, far, far, farrrrrrrrr from our overcrowded and dumpy condo, and, more important, our condo's bathroom. In fact, we were miles away from any real bathroom. I had just been peeing in the lake all day, hoping that nobody noticed.

Our only mode of transport was a party barge that looked like the ones they give away in the Showcase Showdown portion of *The Price Is Right*.[17] Not exactly a vehicle designed for speed. I needed to get to a bathroom ASAP. Couldn't we have taken a cigarette boat or a hovercraft? Did we have to rent this dumb floating rectangle? A garage was more aerodynamic. I started to panic and pulled Sheryle aside to ask for help.

"I need to go, Sheryle."

"Uh-huh. One minute. Kevin wants to show me his swan dive."

Sheryle was having a blast and getting her flirt on with her bicycle man.

"I need to go like NOW."

I could not be the freshman girl who shat in Lake Powell. That was *not* an option. Sheryle begrudgingly asked her crush if he could drive me back to our hotel on our giant raft.

"Kevin said he would drive you back. "

Thank god. Three cheers for Kevin! Kevin steered the Showcase Showdown boat slowly back to safety. I just kept holding my breath and counting to one hundred and back down again, making deals with God to get me to a bathroom.

If you can hear me, God, I will make good choices for the rest of my life. I will not steal my roommate's food anymore and then lie to her face about it when she confronts me. I will be a good person. I know I have never checked in with you before, and my family didn't go to church, but please do me a solid!

I got back to our condo, and I was bright red like a sunburnt lobster. I was bloated with salty tortilla chips, and I was about

---

17. Remember: if you make it to the Showcase Showdown, always go for the trips or the car. Never ever the dumbass "party boat."

to have a private moment that one does not want to have while sharing a bathroom with thirty other people in a condo. Neither my dignity nor my anal virginity were intact. But I made it. I would not have to spend the rest of my college years as the Lake Shitter. Hallelujah!

I decided that the best move for the Unofficial Grand Chancellor of Personal Safety from now on was to stay in my parents' basement, put on *Queer Eye*, and try to make eye contact with the UPS guy.

Please, Call Me Mrs. Myrin

If you are going to spend eternity six feet under, why not be buried with your favorite vice and a dress with a thigh-high slit? Just because you're not a fox in life doesn't mean that you're not going to be a hot commodity in the hereafter.

When I got the call that my father's mother, Granny Helen, had passed away, it was sort of an odd feeling. While I was never as close to her as I was with my mom's mother, Hilda, I appreciated Granny's swagger and wanted to honor her in the afterworld. She was part of the original Hasty Decisions Club—the first of my direct descendants to marry on a whim. Hilda and Harry were in love. Helen and Lars had just met.

My maternal grandmother, Grandma Hilda, was cuddly and cute. She would bake you a birthday cake, needlepoint you a pillow, and teach you how to play cards. Willy's mom, Granny Helen, was not the cute grandma that you see in movies baking pies and telling nursery tales. No, Helen was a true broad, and she had *swagger*.

While Helen was a vaguely scary lady who looked like she was eighty when she was actually forty, she was fun—fun in the way that grown-ups who don't know how to relate to children are fun. They don't know what to say, so they just treat you like a tiny adult. By the time I was five, we had really hit our stride.

"Arden, can you make me a Bloody Mary?"

Can I???? You bet I can!

Because she had taught me! Granny was the kind of woman who could rock a turban and teach you how to garnish a Tom Collins. One always got the feeling that she had forgotten it was your birthday, so whatever present she gave you was usually unwrapped and most likely something she just dug out of her alligator handbag that day. Lighters, an old piece of costume jewelry, a half-eaten roll of butterscotch hard candies—all of these were proper birthday gifts to be given to people young and old.

The prize trinket that came out of her handbag was on my seventh birthday. Grandma Helen showed up to my party rocking a fabulous, short Pucci A-line dress. It was like seeing a skeleton in a micro mini. I had a collection of beloved rubber ink stamps that I would put all over my schoolwork; think teddy bears, hearts, and stars. These all got thrown to the wayside when I received the *greatest gift ever given to a second grader in the history of mankind*!!! A rubber stamp that read: BEEFEATER MARTINI ON ROCKS WITH LEMON TWIST.

I didn't know what it was, but I knew that I loved it. It didn't even require a separate inkpad; it had its *own* inkpad that lived with it. As an adult, I realize that it is alarming that Granny had such a need to order that specific drink that she had commissioned a stamp to be made. Did she think it would take far too long for a waiter to write it down?

Oh, how I loved that stamp! Where did she even get it? I put it everywhere! Letters and notes, doodles and drawings. I proudly put that martini stamp all over my notebooks and my schoolwork. I was certain that Mrs. Drake, my fourth-grade teacher at the Wilbur School, would be as dazzled by my capacity to order a drink as my ability to spell the word *terrarium*. I guessed wrong.

The greatest gift for a seven-year-old of all time!

Apparently, Mrs. Drake found it "inappropriate" and "unsettling." Her loss. Not everyone appreciates high levels of glamour and sophistication. I may have lived in a farm town, but I had visions of growing up and going to El Morocco or the 21 Club in Manhattan and ordering my special drink.

One afternoon, Granny came over for a visit and announced that she was going to make me a grilled cheese sandwich. Didn't seem like an odd declaration to me; Grandma Hilda made me grilled cheeses all the time. But it became quickly obvious by watching her that Helen Myrin had never cooked a thing in her life.

Granny started by heating up a half stick of butter in a frying pan. So far so good; butter is always my friend. Then she pulled out a loaf of Wonder Bread and a stack of American cheese and seemed totally stumped.[18] My mother was watching the whole proceeding warily.

"Do you need help, Mrs. Myrin?"

Mrs. Myrin.

Granny never once said to my mom, "Please, call me Helen." Or "Call me Mom, I insist." JJ had to call her Mrs. Myrin until Granny's deathbed.

"I said I can cook it, so I'm going to cook it, Janet."

"You got it, Mrs. Myrin."

My mom made a face behind her back.

Having properly shut down her daughter-in-law, Granny moved on. She put two pieces of Wonder Bread in the toaster and slid a slice of American cheese into the boiling butter stew, where it began floating on top of the sea of fat.

Willy did a drive-by of the kitchen to see what was going on and made himself a bowl of cereal in a gigantic mixing bowl. He poured into it every flavor of cereal our pantry held.

Compared with his mother, Willy was starting to look like Wolfgang Puck. He may have made disgusting concoctions, but at least he could cook (or at least pour things into a bowl).

"Granny's making you lunch?!"

He burst into a combo of a hack and a laugh.

"Good luck!"

He may have been laughing, but that didn't stop him from dipping a finger into the hot butter-cheese combo and pulling out a tidbit of cheese like a finger fondue for himself.

It seemed like eternity that I was stuck waiting for Granny. At one point she pulled out her fancy leather cigarette case that

---

18. Of course, this is the woman who gave birth to Willy Myrin! Look at her cooking skills!

held both a pack of Virginia Slims and a gold lighter. She lit one up and sucked it down. With her right hand occupied by her "ciggy," she used her free left hand to wave the spatula around to express herself as she chatted with me.

"Do you have a boyfriend yet?"

I was five.

"Not yet, Granny."

"Well—it's just as easy to love a rich man as a poor man."

Touché. I didn't know how to respond.

"Thanks for the tip."

Ding! Saved by the bell of the toaster.

Granny pulled out two pieces of toast, put one on a plate, and proceeded to pour the butter-cheese combo onto the bread. The floating slice of heated up American cheese slithered over the side of the pan like a kid on a waterslide. She capped off the sandwich by placing the other piece of toast on top of the drenched slice and handed it over.

"Bon appétit!"

With my lunch taken care of, Granny got out a cereal bowl into which she proceeded to slice up a banana with a butter knife and poured orange juice all over it. She picked at her orange juice–banana soup with a spoon, cigarette still going, and watched me eat my death bomb. She wasn't going to risk gaining weight like me on a butter-cheese diet, no ma'am! Granny needed to be in tip-top shape—she always wanted to look good for men.

Watching television with her over the years was always an interesting event—like getting trapped by Miss Havisham with a remote control. She would sit and tell me how she wanted to be buried (with a cigarette in hand), and what I could have when she died (her lamps). We would then eat popcorn (or at least *I* ate popcorn, and she smoked) and watch *The Tonight Show*. One eight-year-old and one eighty-year-old—night owls side by side on the couch. Convinced she was still the belle of the ball, Granny would watch TV and have to fight off all the imaginary suitors in her brain.

"Johnny Carson now there's a man I wouldn't marry!"

Apparently, just because you don't know a celebrity personally does not mean that he won't propose someday. I couldn't imagine that Johnny Carson was actually banging down her door, but I like that she had a firm stand on things. Granny was obsessed with men, particularly whom she would and would not marry. She was convinced that every man on the planet was clamoring to get in on some hot Helen Myrin action.

"Dean Martin thinks he is the cat's meow. He's not getting a piece of me."

Never mind that Dean Martin had passed away years before.

Granny was always a remote and terrifying presence in my life, but occasionally she would reach out to me in weird and mysterious ways. While I was in college a letter arrived from her. Or rather, I should say an envelope arrived from her with my name on it. Inside there was no letter or card, just a clipping of a cartoon from the *New Yorker*. It had a drawing of two bank safes humping each other with the caption: "Safe sex." Up top, it just read: *Ha. Hope you're having safe sex! Granny.*

It felt like some sick joke that everyone was in on—treating me like I was the Whore of College Babylon when I couldn't even get laid.

When Granny had to be moved into a nursing home, she stashed a carton of Virginia Slims under her mattress. She would get caught and reprimanded, but like the honey badger in the world's greatest YouTube video, Helen didn't give a shit! She would just demand that we bring her a new carton when we would visit. We all knew she'd stuck to her smoking guns, because when she finally passed away, her mattress was riddled with cigarette burns.

Going to visit her at her stinky nursing home in Philly was always an experience of taking your life into your hands. It was not dangerous in the standard nursing home "watch out for the oxygen tank" kind of a way, but rather in the way that she still had access to a car. Granny had an old Lincoln Continental with suicide doors that she called the Black Panther, in which she would throw me, my mother, and Alarik in the back seat. Not a seatbelt to be found, Granny Helen would put the pedal to the metal and rip through the parking lot of her nursing home registering speeds of up to eighty miles per hour. Flying over the speed bumps, Alarik and I would be bouncing around, hitting the roof of the Black Panther. We were giggling and loved it. My mother was as pale as a ghost, clinging on to her brood, trying to keep calm.

"How is the food here, Mrs. Myrin?"

"Who cares."

For decades I thought Granny was one hundred years old, whereas in reality she was probably only fifty-three. Cigarettes, no solid food, and some "mother's little helpers" (1950s lady pills [Valium]) give you nice legs but ages your face well before its time.

When we finally got the call that Granny had passed away, I knew I had to do what she had been preparing me to do for all these years: honor her wishes, making sure she was buried with a cigarette in her hand.

I couldn't let her down.

I have a great respect for doing what you've got to do to make yourself okay with death. And more specifically, being sealed into a coffin and being placed into the earth. Being claustrophobic, I have always had a big fear of accidentally being buried alive. As a kid, I had seen a news program where they interviewed people who actually *had* been buried alive. I became obsessed with preventing it. I looked into a buzzer system to be rigged from my grave in case I had one last breath in me and they had buried me too soon.

When that seemed too complicated, I tried to get Sheryle to sign a legal document agreeing to let me be stuffed and have my bones replaced with pipe cleaners so she could dress me up in cute clothes, change my position, and put jaunty hats on me in the entryway to her home. One day, I could be wearing a sporty nautical look, and another I could rock a Regal Country Squire vibe complete with a monocle and a top hat. Basically, I want to look like a stuffed Mr. Peanut when greeting my visitors.

No one is going to claim that funerals are a good time, but who says they have to be so serious? Why should Egyptian pharaohs be the only ones who get to sail into the afterworld fully stocked? Helen may not have been allowed to smoke or carouse at her nursing home/elder prison, but I was going to make damn sure she was stocked up with Virginia Slims for her party in the great beyond.

Granny passed away in the middle of winter, and they rushed to get her into the ground before another Nor'easter took place. I arrived late to her funeral, as it was an icy, stormy winter day, and I had to fly in from college. I made my way to the graveyard, where the funeral was already in full swing and the casket had long been closed. Oh, shit—I was too late! I pulled my mom aside and whispered in her ear.

"Mom, what about her wish? All she ever told me was that she wanted to be buried with a cigarette in her hand."

We Myrins may be a lot of things, but being disrespectful to a person's vice is not one of them. As the reverend was saying a few words, the Myrins began to quietly rally. Who would have a cigarette? Willy wasn't packing. He had miraculously quit smoking as a gift to my brother for his fourteenth birthday. (Watching him puff out those last few smoke rings was like watching a child get their first taste of ice cream—delighted, in heaven, mesmerized. Willy was really, *really* good at blowing smoke rings.)

Would my uncle who wears a cape while racing antique motorcycles with sidecars up and down the coast of England have a smoke? You would think so, but oddly no. My fabulous aunt who does not wear shoes and has a trapeze from her bedroom to her living room *did* smoke but was not able to make the cross-country trek. Not wanting to be impolite to the deceased, we continued our hunt.

"Reverend—if you could wait a moment, there is one last thing."

The frantic hunt for a cigarette continued until my thirteen-year-old cousin, the Nipper, calmly produced one from his giant overcoat. He was also wearing a black neck warmer as a hat—a two-foot-long fleece stove top hat that stood straight up to the sky with his hair poking out on top like the Muppet Beaker. Would the Nipper's parents be upset that he had a pack of smokes? Nope. His mom, Elin, was happy because she was out of her own cigarettes and wanted one herself. No one batted an eye, relieved that we could honor the dead properly—we had found what Granny wanted.

But then came the tough question: Who would put said cigarette in her hand? As we Myrins are not a very brave group of people, no one wanted to be the one to actually do the deed. So we drew straws. Elin lost. Up came the lid, down went the cigarette into Granny's hand. The Myrins breathed a collective sigh of relief.

After the funeral, everyone had to give props to Helen for coming up with a really good idea. We may not be that organized, but we all started mulling on what trophies from earth we wanted to travel with us on our journey to the afterlife.

We didn't want to be dead drips, so we joked around about what we wanted. My father had his eye on a bottle of Johnny Walker Black scotch, a remote control, and a photo of Heather Locklear in her *T. J. Hooker* days. I said I would throw in an old cookie and a hammer for good measure. Alarik wanted to be buried as a life-size human replica of Han Solo frozen in carbonite (that way they could unfreeze him perfectly when they got the technology). I will be stuffed like a pipe cleaner doll and available to dress up in jaunty outfits and used as a coatrack. And for Janet, I wanted to send her off with the Medal of Valor for sticking it out with all of us.

*   .
 . *
*

Little Miss Little Compton

How did I get from being a "polite young man" in the creamed corn aisle at the local general store to a "TV unfuckable" cast member of the NBC sitcom *Working* at the age of twenty-two? It was mostly thanks to the Grandmaster JJ herself!

To really understand what it means to be "TV unfuckable," think of the wacky redheaded neighbor lady in a crazy cardigan sweater (who stalks the male lead), or the weird office assistant in retro dice earrings and a neckerchief who reads *Cathy* comics (and stalks the male lead). There was even an ad during the height of "Must See TV" that ran during *Seinfeld* for an episode of *Just Shoot Me!* that I had done, in which I played David Spade's character's nerdy dream girl, who was the other woman to Rebecca Romijn (and yes, stalks the male lead). The ad's booming voiceover even asked: "Would you leave Rebecca Romijn for *this* woman??!!!"

The voiceover accompanied a freeze-frame shot of me wearing a gigantic black T-shirt that read: SPOCK ROCKS on it, my hair was in two pigtails on top of my head, and I was making an expression that looked like I was having a seizure.

I didn't get to be TV unfuckable just by having a real knack for seeming like a lonely stalker. Oh, no. There was a whole foundation built by the Grandmaster JJ herself that gave me the proper tools to seem lonely and stalkerish in an artful way.

My mom exposed me to culture (both high and low), encouraged my creativity, believed in me, and taught me to have a work ethic. She worked from the time I was in kindergarten. JJ taught me to balance a spreadsheet, work my ass off, protect my magic, and not to have a "B Plan" (but welcome a side hustle if needed) and *go for it*! Yes, ma'am!

On the other hand, my dad was never outwardly excited by or proud of anything I did. When I moved to LA to be on *Working*, he would cut out and mail me newspaper articles of the twenty-five most popular actresses under the age of twenty-five, with nothing but the words "Where are you?" written on the top. When my first episode of *Working* aired, he never called. Instead, I made the error of calling home the next day.

"Hey, Willy! It's me."

"Yeah."

"Did you see the show?"

"Yeah, I saw it."

"Well . . . what did you think?"

"I thought it stunk. And you stunk with it."

You can see why JJ was my preferred parent. I was twenty-two years old, and I was a series regular on a sitcom having grown up with no comedy or acting connections in the industry. And that was his response. To this day, I still don't know why he was so unkind and hurtful. I know that he probably didn't like himself very much, but his wounding words still cut me to the core. It's unnatural to be so cruel to your offspring.

Fortunately, my mom's light shone so brightly on me and my brother that I didn't let my dad stop me from staying true to myself and pursuing my dreams. As I mentioned before, it just takes one. One human who sees you to give you the courage to try. Even if that human is yourself. You can be your own JJ!

Sometimes you need to shield what is important to you from people who are vultures. From then on, I started to protect what I was proud of around my dad and would keep our conversations to the topics of news, weather, and sports. Since I didn't watch sports and I didn't want to talk politics with him, it was mostly weather.

"Wow! Another hurricane! Huh, whaddaya know!"

It didn't feel great not being able to share successes when I had them with my dad, but I am also a realist and had to accept that at a certain point hoping to get a pat on the back from Willy was like Charlie Brown hoping Lucy wouldn't pull away the football. So I leaned into my mom. She would always be there to hold my football.

Since I was a toddler, Janet could tell I loved comedy. I was a very silly child who was always writing plays and staging them in the living room or in the yard. I would base them on what I had seen on television the night before. Let's just say I watched lots of late-night TV. A natural early bird, Janet would let her two night owl children stay up until the wee hours, making things, reading, daydreaming, watching TV, and filling our brains with possibility.

Starting in second grade, my mom would let me stay up and watch *Saturday Night Live* or would tape it for me and fast-forward through the dirty parts. She had great taste in pop culture and would show me Gilda Radner and Lily Tomlin, *Animal House* and *Blues Brothers*, Mel Brooks and Madeline Kahn, and Teri Garr. From the age of five, she would take me and my brother to see every Steve Martin movie in the theater. We watched tapes of Monty Python movies and listened to Eddie Murphy albums.

I'm sure none of it was appropriate for an elementary school child, but I *loved* it. All of those performers helped build me. They gave me something to aim for.

Little Compton only had three TV stations well into the '90s (until we got cable), and one of those stations had a local show called *Dialing for Dollars* that would regularly play nothing but old black-and-white movies. I watched them all, enrapt. I wanted to be like Nick and Nora in the *Thin Man*, or Judy Holliday or a Busby Berkeley musical dame who hung out at the Rainbow Room and worked as a cigarette girl while waiting for my dreams to come true.

It helped that my mom didn't care if my brother and I got straight A's or went to fancy colleges; she just wanted us to figure out what made our tails wag, protect it, and use that as a marker for what we should do in life. She also had one rule for both of her kids—we had to live in New York City for two years, and after that we could do whatever we wanted. She saw New York City as the land of opportunity; whatever your dreams were, if you could harness that magical Big Apple energy, the road would rise to meet you.

Living in New York for two years was fine by me! My favorite show at the age of nine was *Fame*, about LaGuardia High School of Music & Art and Performing Arts in New York. When a young Debbie Allen appears in the opening credits as a stern but fair dance teacher clutching a wooden staff and whipping her dancers into shape, all I wanted to do was get my ass to the city, enroll in her class, and prove to her that I WAS WILLING TO PAY IN SWEAT to get discovered!!!

The bright lights and big city was where it felt like it was all happening. This lined up nicely with the fact that I was exhausted in school because I was a mesmerized fifth grader who stayed up watching David Letterman drop watermelons and bowling balls off the top of buildings. *That was a job? People could do that for a living?!* To hell with algebra—let's move to New York! Give me a bowling ball and a roof to throw it off of! ASAP!!! Unfortunately, JJ insisted that I finish school first before I started my NYC residency.

Starting in kindergarten, my mom would take me and Alarik down to Manhattan on annual trips to expose us to the outside world. She would take us for rides on the subways, showing us all the colorful graffiti.

"Look what people can make with a can of spray paint!"

Mom would take us to see all the lights (and the sex workers) of Times Square at night.

"Those are ladies of the night! Watch them shine!"

We would go to Trader Vic's for giant blue Polynesian mocktails and Benihana to watch the shrimp fly into the chef's pockets. We would go look at the magical window displays at Bergdorf Goodman and would ride the escalators to the top floor to look out their bathroom windows. My mom would exclaim without fail, "Look at that! That's a multimillion-dollar view of the city for free! There's Central Park, and that's the Plaza, where Eloise lived. I'd take you there, but they put booze in their cakes."

She didn't care about the alcohol factor, she just didn't like how their cakes tasted. Janet was a cake purist. No booze in her sweets.

My favorite part of the trip to New York was when my mom would go to the TKTS booth and get half-priced tickets for musicals and take us to Broadway shows. Oh, how I loved musicals! I loved the grand theaters and how everybody dressed up. After the shows, I would run around collecting bags of all the playbills that people had left on their seats, dumbfounded that anyone could leave such treasures behind. The first play I ever saw was when I was four years old—*Annie*. A little on the nose, I know. But *IT. BLEW. MY. MIND.* Seeing a little ginger girl just like me tearing it up on stage was a game changer. I was *hooked. That was it for me.* I needed to be Little Orphan Annie!!!!

Trips to Manhattan with JJ and my brother felt like how Dorothy must have felt when she got to Oz. The lights switched on in my brain and life became Technicolor! It was like a lighthouse beam in the night. There was a whole world of magic out there just waiting for me! I just had to figure out how to get from my bedroom in the middle of a hayfield to a soundstage in Manhattan or Hollywood.

I started to hatch a plan of escape from small town living after I met a girl named Rebecca, an adorable and very sweet little child who moved down the road from me when I was in second grade and she was in kindergarten.

I was *so jealous* of Rebecca. She had moved from New York City. Her dad was an actor, and he had gotten a commercial agent for Rebecca and her brother. A real-life commercial agent! I *could not believe* how glamorous and exciting that was. It was as if Jennifer Lawrence had just moved in a half mile away from me.

Everything about Rebecca was mesmerizing. I grilled her about her agent, life in the big city, what it was like auditioning, and her biggest triumph—acting in a Life cereal commercial. She enjoyed the filming but didn't like giving some strange lady playing her mom a kiss on the cheek, take after take. Rebecca made her own money and had a bank account and got to skip school, and to top it all off, she got to eat bowl after bowl of Life

Little Miss Little Compton

cereal *at work*—which she did not enjoy. Whatttttt???? What
the hell was wrong with her? Cereal is delicious! (Cereal would
eventually make me gain twenty pounds my freshman year in
college.) But I'm not a monster. I love to eat cereal! Sign me up!

Rebecca could also cry on cue. I know this because her mom
used to tell my mom that fact repeatedly.

"Rebecca's SUCH a little actress. She can cry on cue."

My blood boiled. I couldn't (and still can't) cry on cue. But
I could (and still can) do the Worm, and that seemed like a
perfectly good substitute. I felt so sorry for Rebecca that she
had to move to the country, where no one came knocking when
casting a new Count Chocula commercial. It was official—at
that moment I knew it was my destiny to become a professional
working, cereal-eating actress. As beautiful as Little Compton
was, I had to GET THE HELL OUT OF DODGE, get me an
agent, and get GOING!

I would sit JJ down and explain to her that she was holding
back my career and that we needed to move to NY or LA *now*
so I could get an agent and pursue my dreams. She wanted me
to live there eventually anyway; what was the difference? But my
mom wouldn't budge and refused to uproot the entire family to
service a seven-year-old with stars in her eyes.

"As soon as you are old enough to not get kidnapped when
you move alone to a big city, have at it. You can become my
little cash cow. Until then, stay in school."

Fine.

I buckled down and decided to grow where I was planted.
I was lucky enough to go to a high school where we had a nice
stage. Unfortunately, Dale, the keeper of the stage (and the
head of the theater department), was not a fan of mine. At all.

164

Dale was a stern woman with a very practical haircut who kept trying to distract me from "nonsense" like *Little Shop of Horrors* with written assignments of breaking down *Hedda Gabler* beat by beat. Which I'll admit was probably useful, but boorrrrring. We get it: there's a gun in the first act and it's going to go off by the end of act three. Spoiler alert. DUH.

Dale was assigned to me as my faculty advisor and would chain-smoke cigarettes indoors and glare at me through the smoky haze during our meetings.

"Do you have to be so louuuud?"

Dale rarely let me be in any of the plays, although she did cast me as Fat Jan in our production of *Grease*. Perhaps she cast me because she could sense my Life cereal-eating skills. I aimed to wow her as I shoveled can after can of cold SpaghettiOs down my gullet on stage. Didn't work. Despite my ability to happily eat prop food, Dale wasn't buying what I was selling.

Which was one of the best things that ever happened to me.

Because if I had been easily cast, I wouldn't have had to pivot and use my JJ Jedi warrior skills to protect my magic and go for my dreams despite all the obstacles. I was on a mission. I needed to get around stern Dale. So I built my own boat.

My school had an annual One Act Play Festival in which students would find old one act plays from library books or pull scenes from well-known plays and stage them in a competition. To get around my nemesis, I decided to write my own play. Starting sophomore year, I wrote, directed, and acted in a play each year for the festival. I wouldn't have had the fire in my belly to do it if I had just been cast in the productions.

Starting to make my own creations made me happier than anything I had ever done in my life. Eventually, creating my own shows started to be what I was known for. For the first time in my life, I felt like I made sense. Dale didn't like it, but I didn't care. I was on a mission.

To anyone else out there who has dreams of performing, I say just start making things. Anything—movies on your phone, stand-up in a coffee shop, performances in a friend's yard. Anything. Just start building your own boat, because that is where the magic is.

As I got older and started applying to colleges, my mom encouraged me to protect what was unique about me. Watching how happy I was staging my own plays, she actually encouraged me to *not* go to theater school. She sensed that what was special about me might not be what was appreciated at a place like Julliard (if I could even get in).

She thought I would be a more well-rounded person if I went to a liberal arts school, which would make me a better performer and writer. Her theory was that since I was lucky enough to know what I wanted to do for a living and that I was hopefully going to do that for the rest of my life, I would be a happier and more interesting person if I took four years to learn about lots of different things in the world and meet different kinds of people.

I took her advice and went to a liberal arts college. As you know, I hated it. Big time. It was a perfectly good school, just the wrong school for me. And that turned out to be another one of the biggest gifts of my life, because, again, I had to pivot.

I had to be scrappy. I couldn't afford to transfer (because they wouldn't take my credits), so I figured out a way to educate myself *and* get college credits for the things that seemed interesting to me. I went to Chicago and got an internship at ImprovOlympic. It was a miracle I ended up working there. Everyone in the arts program I was in had to interview at five places before choosing where they wanted to work.

After four interviews, I decided to intern for an actress who had a successful theater career and had a few lines in movies. I was over the moon but looking back it had the potential to be a total *nightmare*. She kept making jokes about how excited she was to have someone go get her dry cleaning and someone she could send out for her special clove cigarettes. I didn't care. I wanted to see a real live actress in action, but I had one more interview to go before I committed.

That interview was with Charna Halpern at the ImprovOlympic Theater that she founded with improv guru Del Close (which has since been renamed the iO Theater). At the time, I had only been exposed to one type of improv, that of a cheesy short form college improv troupe. The troupe seemed to always be performing the game Freeze in the student center. ("Freeze! Mr. Anderson get your hand off my ass!") So I wasn't that interested. That all changed after Charna encouraged me to go watch the improv shows that night. So, begrudgingly, I went.

My mind was blown. The house team at the time—The Family—consisted of future Oscar winner and *Anchorman* writer and director Adam McKay, future UCB cofounders Ian Roberts and Matt Besser, future The Pit Theater cofounder Ali Farahnakian, future star of every sitcom ever Neil Flynn, and the brilliant Miles Stroth. I could not believe my eyes. It was the most exciting show I had ever seen performed live.

I saw two shows that night doing two formats of long-form improv. The first was a brilliantly performed Harold.[19] The other show I saw was a new format they were working on that was a long-form fully improvised movie complete with descriptions of camera angles, cutaways, and music improvised and scored live on the piano by Jeff Richmond—a genius who would go on to write music for *30 Rock* and *Mean Girls* the musical. The performers at iO were *so* good, and it was thrilling to see what was possible. Finally, I felt like I had found my tribe.

I immediately told the actress that I couldn't intern for her, and I called Charna and officially became the first ever intern at iO. I soaked up as much as I could. Charna was very kind to me and let me take all the classes for free. All of them. At once. I just dove in and took beginning, intermediate, and advance class (taught by Del Close) simultaneously. Looking back, I probably should have gone in order, starting with just beginner first, and learned my ABCs of improv. I was out of my league in the more advanced levels since I had not learned the basics yet, but I just wanted to learn as much as I could as fast as I could.[20]

At the time, the shows were performed in a small space above the Wrigleyside, a sports bar in Wrigleyville, Chicago, a few blocks from Wrigley Stadium. I was only nineteen at the time, so I got my hands on a fake ID so I could get into the bar to sell the tickets and watch the shows. I was there watching

---

19. The Harold is an improv show that is broken up into three acts, with three scenes each. By the end of the piece, all of the three scenes have started to weave together. When done well, it makes you feel like you have witnessed a well-written spontaneous play.

20. I was always aware that I didn't learn it in the proper order and felt a little bit ashamed about that, so a few years later I would go through the entire program in the proper order, starting at Level 1, when they opened a branch in LA.

shows every night the theater was open, mesmerized by what people could create together.

I had never been around so many funny people in my life. The people that were in Chicago at that time whom I got to hang out with as a nineteen-year-old was astounding—future *Colbert Report* writer Laura Kraft; future *SNL* stars Horatio Sanz, Rachel Dratch, and Dave Koechner; and Adult Swim star Jon Glaser. Amy Poehler arrived just after I left and killed it there. Adam McKay was (and remains to this day) the funniest person I have ever met in my entire life.

Adam McKay hanging out with a nineteen-year-old version of yours truly at a party in Chicago in the '90s.

It was incredible. It was one of the happiest years of my life. But at the time it was also very male. Everyone was very nice to me and so funny, but it's hard to imagine how you'll shine when you don't look like the other people on the stage. I was also still a teenager, so it was hard for me to imagine how I would thrive in that environment. I know now it was possible because Amy Poehler did it shortly after I left.

I think I wanted to please all those guys so badly and make them think that I was good and funny that I knew it was not the right place for me to find my own voice. I wanted their validation too much. But it was my second lighthouse signal (after going to NYC as a child) that there were people like me out there doing their thing and thriving. I remember I told Charna that my dream was to be on *Saturday Night Live*, and she told me, "Oh, honey, shoot bigger than that."

I will always be grateful to Charna and Chicago for exposing me to the most concentrated group of talented people I have ever been around in my life. I feel so lucky I got to witness all of these amazing comedic minds right before they launched and took over TV and movies. It was one of the happiest years of my life.

Financially, it was going to be hard for me to go back to school that fall, so I figured out a way to get credit if I moved to New York and got an internship at a TV show. I applied to thirty places and only one wrote me back—a brand new (and at the time struggling) TV show called *Late Night with Conan O'Brien*. I immediately took it, found the cheapest shithole of an apartment I could get my hands on, and begged my friend Katie to come with me and split rent. I got paid in subway tokens and would steal food from the snack area after guests had left behind their cheese plates.

It was amazing to be on that show at the very beginning, partly because it was so new that all the good interns went to *Letterman*. So if you were competent at all, you got to move up and have some responsibility. I was assigned to the script supervisor, a wondrous woman named Brenda Ventura who was from Brooklyn. Upon meeting me, she exclaimed, "Ah-den? What the FUCK kind of name is that? With your long blond hair, looking at me like I'm some kind of gindaloon with my long red nails and my big fucking tits."

I didn't know what a gindaloon was, but I did know that I was IN LOVE. I *loved* working with Brenda. She made me laugh and was amazing at her job, and was protective of me.

"If anybody touches a hair on your head, I know guys. They will drag their faces along the pavement."

Wow! Toto! We're not in Little Compton anymore!

The beauty of working for Brenda meant that I got to spend my mornings up in the *Conan* productions offices at 30 Rock seeing how a TV show ran behind the scenes. In the afternoons, I would accompany Brenda a few floors down to the stage for rehearsals in case there were any changes made to the script. Robert Smigel was the head writer at the time and was brilliant (although Brenda would get frustrated with him for turning in page after page of handwritten notes that she could barely read for sketches like the "Masturbating Bear" and "The Year 2000." She was never frustrated for long because he was so hilarious).

During the show, I got to sit in the control room next to Brenda and see how a show is called from the director in the control room. It was thrilling. To be far away from the fields of my youth and in a real-live TV studio was as eye-opening and inspiring as I had hoped it would be.

When my time ended there, they very kindly offered me a job as a PA. There was only one problem. What I really wanted was to be one of the guests on the show. I had to bet on myself. Three years later I *would* be a guest on *Late Night with Conan O'Brien*, an event that really made me feel like my dreams were coming true. They even played the *Welcome Back, Kotter* theme song. It was so wonderful.

*Being a guest on Conan in 1997 was one of the
first times I really felt like I had made it. It was a joy.*

I went back to school and did two years in a year so I could
graduate on time. I took every half and quarter credit I could to
make it happen. I became a certified basketball coach, learned
to play the drums, and directed a musical. I did what I could to
land the education plane on time and on budget—and I did!
I was ready to fulfill JJ's requirement and got my ass to New
York City!

Two weeks after graduation, Sheryle and I loaded a U-Haul
filled with Goodwill couches and chairs that I had staple-gunned
zebra fabric all over. We lucked out and rented an apartment
for a thousand bucks one block from Central Park. I hunted
down Mikie Heilbrun, the casting director from *Conan*, who
hooked me up with an internship for anther casting director,
Bonnie Finnegan. Bonnie is a wonderful casting director, and
her associate Beth Bowling really helped educate me about the
process of auditioning.

It was fascinating. I would watch some of the actors come in for pilots and see them try to psych each other out in the waiting room, not realizing that the producers were on the ninth day of casting and that the competition truly was not with the other people in the waiting room but really against themselves.

Sometimes Bonnie would let me be the reader, and I learned so much watching the audition styles of all the people who came in for various parts. It was so helpful learning how to behave beyond just the actual audition. I highly recommend to any aspiring actors out there to be a reader for a casting director if given the chance.

Some people would come in and talk about themselves for so long before they started that they shot themselves in the foot before they even said one line. I learned to be gracious and prepared and chatted a little if it was initiated, but to also not be a time goblin[21] in the room.

I also learned that sometimes the person who does the best audition does not get the part. For whatever reason the powers that be want a redhead, or they hate redheads, or you remind them of their sister who they love, or you remind them of their sister who they hate. It is not personal. Be prepared, be on time, don't be chaos. I also always try to make a strong choice when auditioning; it may not be what they are looking for, but hopefully it will stand out and they can always give you an adjustment for the character and have you try the audition again in a slightly different way.

My friend Andy Flemming said that one of his favorite things that his mom used to say was, "Don't give 'em what they want. Make 'em want what you've got." That's what I try to

---

21. A person who steals other people's time.

do with auditions. (Thanks for sharing this with me, precious American Treasure Andy!)

When I was working for Bonnie, I needed cash. So I would either waitress at night or be an elf at Santaland on the weekends, and on the off nights I would do stand-up. I was terrified of stand-up, but I did it because there is a catch-22.

As an actor, in order to get on stage you need an agent, and in order to get an agent you need to get on stage, so the best way for me to do that was to start doing stand-up. Also, I knew there were not a lot of young ladies who were doing stand-up in the mid-nineties and that I could write for myself. Add that to the fact that I wanted to do comedic acting, so stand-up felt like my best chance to dive into that world.

I performed at Stand-Up New York, The Boston Comedy Club, and the New York Comedy Club, where I met Zach Galifianakis and one of my future BFFs, Lisa DeLarios. I wasn't a great stand-up at twenty-one—I was too terrified of it to excel, but I forced myself to do it anyway, five minutes at a time.

At one of those shows, all of the seeds I had been planting in my career started to grow. Beth Bowling (the casting director who worked with Bonnie) knew a young assistant named Jonathan Bluman at the talent agency Paradigm. I had already sent my headshot to them and they had passed on me, but Beth invited Jonathan to one of my stand-up shows and we hit it off.

Jonathan was a few years older than me and he didn't have any clients, but he was a blast and cool and he got me. He had a buddy at ABC in casting named Jeremy Gold, and he set up a general meeting for us, sort of like a meet and greet. Jeremy and I hit it off and he told me there was a part he wanted me to come in for on a new pilot called *Daisy's Mom*. It was the part of the wacky babysitter, and it was in my wheelhouse. I was twenty-one and had a red bob haircut, I wore bright red lipstick and had a closetful of vintage cardigan sweaters, and I was a silly young lady. "Wacky babysitter" was just the kind of part I could book. Believe it or not, this one did not require me to stalk the male lead!

I worked really hard on my audition and tried to apply everything I had been learning while working for Bonnie. I made a strong choice, I didn't chat too much or too little, and I tried to make 'em want what I got. The first audition I was terrified, but it went well and I got a callback. And then I got another one. I kept going in, round after round. I am so grateful that they called me back in for that pilot seven times. Eventually, casting called and wanted to put together a test deal for me and fly me to LA for a test at Warner Brothers and ABC.

Off I went with my little suitcase. I wasn't old enough to rent a car, and Uber didn't exist yet, so it was a lot of odd taxis driving me around (I even got a ride from an actress I met at an audition who adopted me for the day and who ended up being Ana Gasteyer). I went in to test, and after getting approved by Warner Brothers I was sent to ABC the next day.

At the time, ABC did their tests in a giant room that felt like a theater, with these huge leather Spock chairs. I was the only person who had made it to the final round for the part and . . . I did not get it.[22] But me testing for my first audition ever did get me signed by Paradigm. And I am so grateful that once

---

22. I have since tested numerous times for pilots where I am the only person testing for a part and have still not gotten it. My friend Steve Hytner says it's the kiss of death. The powers that be like to have a choice.

Jonathan signed me on as his first client, we were off to the races. I quickly booked an AMC show and a few movies.

Me and my first agent, Jonathan Bluman, backstage at Conan.

I decided to go spend three months in Los Angeles for pilot season, where I actually lived in the closet of Zach Galifianakis and his best friend, who he called Albaldo because Zach thought he looked like a balding albino. I'm not trying to brag, but it was pretty glamorous sleeping on a secondhand air mattress that had a slow leak in it. Every night I would fill up my bed with the vacuum cleaner and get ready to count the sheep in my weird little alcove.

I drove a car from Rent-A-Wreck that always pulled to the left, which was good because my neck and posture were so fucked up from basically sleeping on a half-filled inner tube that it compensated for the fact that my car wanted to drive me straight into a ditch. It also had no air conditioning, so I would have to drive to all my auditions with rolls of toilet paper stuck into the armpits of my shirt on account of my nerves, just so that I wouldn't show up with huge pit stains before I even walked in the door.

But the angels were watching over me, and at the very end of my three-month tenure I was about to go back to New York.

I had tested for a few pilots but not booked anything, and my dad had just had a bad heart attack. I felt like it was best if I went home. My agents asked me to give them one more week of trying. There was a pilot for an NBC sitcom called *Working* that had been floating around a few months. I know this because Zach had gone in to audition for a part on the show in early February.

There was one part they could not cast, that of Abby Cosgrove, a woman in her late thirties who makes C-section jokes about having her second child. Not exactly the perfect fit for this spritely twenty-two-year-old, *but* they were looking and had not yet found the right person for the part. They agreed to see me and were open to making the character a little younger. I ended up auditioning seven separate times for the part before booking it my last day in LA. HALLELUJAH!!! My inner five-year-old went as crazy as the girl from *Little Miss Sunshine* when I got the call that I got the part. Zach heard me squealing and asked why I was so loud. All of a sudden I was Little Miss Little Compton!

Working on *Working* was the BEST! It became the real beginning of my professional career, and I got to work with three people who would become some of my best friends: Fred Savage, Dana Gould, and Steve Hytner. And the biggest miracle of all was that one of our main directors, Jamie Widdoes's wife, was also from Little Compton. I KNOW! CRAZYYYY, RIGHT!!!???

Jamie knew how far I had come and was protective of me; he was patient with the fact that I did not understand camera blocking or how to hold a prop in the same hand take after take for continuity. He knew I could never have learned these things at Wilbur's General Store. I felt like I had a lucky star guiding and watching over me. My wish had come true.

We filmed the pilot for Working *for twenty-four hours straight. This was at six a.m., when we finally wrapped. My costar, Sarah Knowlton, and I celebrated outside the Sunset Gower Studios.*

I was in my early twenties and on a sitcom. I didn't quite realize the magic of just starting out and thought it would always be so easy to book things. Not so. It gets a little trickier when you are no longer the brand-new kid in town. BUT thanks to JJ, I know how to pivot and buckle down and make some of my own magic when needed. Improv, stand-up, writing, podcasting—all of these I started in between jobs to stay busy and make money, and have turned out to be where I've met most of my friends and are a huge part of my career.

A Polaroid of me and Fred Savage in my dressing room at Working.

In any medium it's good to be able to build your own boat— it keeps you sharp and helps you have a hand in showing people what you are capable of. And more important, it shows yourself that you already have everything you need inside of you.

Delayed Reactions

It is an amazing thing to witness a world where it is becoming more normal and more acceptable for people to speak up when they are harassed. With so many people coming forward with their personal stories, people often ask, "Why didn't they leave in the moment?" or "Why didn't they report them?" I can tell you from my experience, it is complicated. I am stunned at how difficult it still is for me to stand up for myself. I never seem to have the right words at the right time. But I am learning by witnessing so many amazing, brave people that it is okay to hold others accountable for their actions.

I have spoken up for myself twice recently. Both times were terrifying—I still didn't want to be a bother. Both times I tried to convince myself that I was being uptight, or that it wasn't that big of a deal—I didn't want people to be mad at me. But I did speak up, and it was uncomfortable and necessary and unpleasant and, ultimately, incredibly freeing.

In both instances, I did not speak up in the moment. I am always so shocked when something has happened to me that I never seem to have the perfect comeback or words to set a boundary in real time. I used to think that if I didn't deal with something right as it was occurring, that I'd missed the opportunity to set a boundary or to stand up for myself. I think one of the biggest things I have learned in adulthood is that it is okay for those of us who are too shocked to speak up in the moment to have delayed reactions—it is okay to set a boundary after the fact. I didn't know this when I first started out.

Early in my career, I booked a small part in a movie that shot in Vegas, which meant I would be there for three and a half weeks, of which I worked a grand total of four days. I was so excited! My first big experience being "on location" coupled with the glamour of Vegas—what could go wrong?

The first day of work I showed up and met the director, a young rocker named Billy who never wore anything but leather pants. Beware of a man who wears leather pants in scorching heat. The movie was an edgy teen movie, the kind of thing I never got to do. I was so excited to bond with the cast and set off on a month-long Vegas bender. It was a super-small cast, and I was the only non-movie star. I envisioned myself as the Shirley MacLaine to their Rat Pack, filming during the days, and then getting past the red velvet ropes with my new celebrity BFFs at night.

It was a pretty quick first morning for me. I shot a scene that lasted about five seconds in the movie—with me standing outside of a mall waving to a car from afar. No one else was in the scene with me, but I didn't care—it was a nice, easy warmup for the rest of the film. I figured I would meet the rest of the cast later, or the next time I worked.

With that I was put on hold for a few weeks. I was set to work the last three days of the shoot, but there were a few scenes Billy was thinking about adding me into, so they decided to keep me in Vegas "just in case." Each morning I would wait for the call from a production assistant to see if Billy was going to use me in the shot that day. He never did. Instead, I had three weeks solo in Vegas, gearing up to work with people I had never met.

I did not count on the fact that movie stars would never stay in the shithole of a hotel I was lodged in, which meant they were no doubt in a fancier hotel across town, so I wouldn't even have the chance to bump into them in the lobby. As it was, I found myself totally alone in a rundown Las Vegas hotel with nothing but time on my hands. I decided to make the best of it! Janet Myrin did not raise a drip! I was going to explore Sin City, but there was one big constriction on my Vegas adventure aside from not having a companion: cash.

When you are in a company town, best to support the local economy! I began my solo tour of Vegas doing what Sin City does best—gambling. Since my Grandma Hilda had taught me to play card games very aggressively, I was confident that I could get the hang of gambling and strike it rich in my time off.

I headed down to the casino. It was noon on a Tuesday, but the place was lit up like it was the Fourth of July. The dingy room was packed with families and Nickel Nuts—the chain-smoking retirees who parked themselves, their walkers, and their buckets of nickels in front of the nickel slot machines. Taking a cue from them, I bought $200 of the smallest denomination chips I could get, to extend my time in the casino. I didn't want to blow it all in one bet! It was a lot of money, but I was confident I could double it in no time.

Getting cocky, I decided to try to learn something new. I had seen the movie *Casino* and thought craps seemed sexy and social. Also, statistically, craps was supposed to be the game with the best odds to win big. Sexy, interacting with other people, and good odds of raking in some dough? Sign me up!

Day one was a rude awakening. Imagining I could be Sharon Stone, a vision of pure glamour blowing on dice and hanging out with Robert DeNiro, I strutted up to the table. Instead of DeNiro, I was greeted by low-rolling octogenarians and their oxygen tanks. I was passed a set of dice by a woman in hot pink shorts and a toucan tank top who looked like she had listened to a lot of Jimmy Buffett songs in her day.

"What do I do?"

Toucan Tank looked at me like I was crazy.

"What do you think? Roll them."

I did not expect that I would have to channel my inner Sharon Stone so quickly. Having never played craps before, I tried to launch the dice with some pizazz.

"Big money! Big money!" I shouted as I tossed them off.

An old man in a baseball hat with an eagle on it glared at me. I had not actually gambled in public before. Turns out, I got most of my gambling smack talk from watching *The Price Is Right*.

Snake eyes. The table was pissed. I passed the dice on to Eagle Hat.

"Sorry. Want me to blow on them for luck?"

"Not your kind of luck."

Eagle Hat snatched the dice from my hand and tossed off what appeared to be a good roll, as everyone around the table high-fived and collected chips. I had no idea how the game was played or what I was betting on, but I enjoyed high-fiving and joined in the fun.

"Woo-hoo! Good roll!"

My strategy at first was to just toss chips down into random boxes and repeat what I heard other people saying.

"Double down! Push the line!"

I did not know what I was talking about. The game continued and my luck seemed to come and go. Mostly go. I stuck pretty close with Eagle Hat and bet small amounts on whatever he put down. He never talked to me, but I felt like we were a team. I thought I could fit in if I silently parroted his craps table confidence.

Eagle Hat was smoking Pall Malls, so I chain-smoked right alongside him. I was not a smoker, but I was just so wowed I could smoke *inside* a building. Side by side, he and I drank watered-down cocktails and passed a good ten to twelve silent minutes together, the exact amount of time it took for me to lose all my money.

The craps game was going fast, and it was confusing. I could just make out random phrases and would shout along with them.

"Box cars! Hi-Lo-Yo! Little Joe!"

When I got the dice again, I panicked. The rest of the table seemed to be on a roll. Right out of the gate I had been a massive disappointment, so I didn't want to let Eagle Hat down. I took the dice, shook them, blew on them, and heard myself shouting: "No whammies!"

Aggressively, I tossed them off hard, causing one die to go flying off the end of the table. The dealer quickly whipped out a new set of dice and handed them to me.

"Thank you."

I took them from him and this time rolled more delicately.

"Same dice! Same dice!"

Now Toucan Tank was in an uproar because I had accepted new, untested (aka "unlucky") dice. I didn't know I was committing a craps faux pas—apparently you stick with hot dice! But it was too late—I had already panicked and thrown the new tainted dice to a pretty lame roll.

I overheard a woman say to her friend, "What's wrong with her?"

The white-haired troops were getting restless. I had never had so many old people be so angry with me. I had started out with five-dollar chips and in the blink of an eye had lost $200 rolling shitty numbers. My career as a professional craps master was evaporating before my eyes.

I would like to say that I quietly left the table and cashed in my chips, but having no chips left to cash in, I gathered up my watered-down Sea Breeze and my empty wallet and slinked off. I am pretty sure I heard a collective exhale from the table as I left. Or maybe that was just their oxygen tanks relaxing a little bit. Eagle Hat did not even say goodbye.

My grand total I was set to earn filming the movie was about $2,700, and craps had made it clear that if I wanted to walk away with any money in my pocket, I had to learn how to do something with my time other than gamble. I headed out for a walk to come up with a game plan on how to spend my remaining twenty-three days in Vegas without bankrupting myself. Surely, fresh air would help me regroup. That is when I learned that if you value your life, don't ever go outside during the day in Vegas.

We shot around Labor Day, which meant that on average the outdoor temperature was a kiln-like 180 degrees, and inside was an air-conditioned minus 3 degrees. This drastic difference in temperature gives you a permanent sore throat—or "Vegas throat," as the locals call it. I had never heard of Vegas throat, but it didn't sound like something I wanted to catch. I also discovered that the sun wants to kill you. As soon as you walk outside, your skin gets seared right off your face.

When I first got to Vegas, it appeared to be the perfect city to conform to my nocturnal body clock, but I didn't know I would be entering hell. My internal clock, which is already pretty ass-backward, went into overdrive. Day became night and night became day. With no windows to the outside world, I never could tell what day or time it was in Vegas. By the fourth day, a person can really start to question their life choices and humanity. By day five, civilization as you know it looks like it is on a rapid downward spiral that will not end well.

Everything in the casino seems designed to keep you discombobulated enough to make bad decisions, but not so unhinged that you actually pass out. Between the watered-down free drinks and the oxygen being pumped in to the casino, I was always vaguely disoriented. Even the rugs started to make me dizzy—all the patterns on the carpets of the casino would give me vertigo and make me woozy. I found myself either wanting to gamble or make out with a guy wearing bedazzled Ed Hardy jeans. I didn't know who I was anymore. Add to that my total lack of human contact, the constant stimulation of lights, the sounds from the nonstop slot machines, and the cigarette haze indoors, and I was a hot mess.

It always felt like it was about 4 a.m. and I was trapped in some kind of jet lag with no one to talk to and no way out. Each morning, the phone would ring and I would answer it, hoping that I would be called to set, but each day Billy kept putting me "on hold" for one more day. Fuck, Billy! I was now mad at Vegas *and* Billy! It was like the movie *Groundhog Day*, but all I was repeating was my insanity. While normally I love some alone time, this was getting creepy and annoying. I was lonely. I had not had a conversation with another human being in days. It didn't help that I would get little "reports" about the action on the set from the production assistant who would call every day.

"This shoot is insane!! Billy is totally out of control."

Apparently, Billy was on some kind of hooker and cocaine bender that was making the studio executives a little nervous. At least one of us was having fun.

Meanwhile, I was getting weirder and weirder. I did a little intervention on myself and forced my body to walk outside. I knew I needed to get some light into my eyes. Having learned from my brief stint at a sleep clinic about those people in Scandinavia who throw themselves to their deaths into fjords in the middle of winter due to lack of natural light, I decided to brave the great outdoors. Maybe if I was in water, I could handle my enemy the sun. I decided to test out whatever pools I could sneak into at various hotels.

You want to feel like a creeper? Try going alone, *without a child*, to the Family Style Lazy River at the Circus-Circus Hotel and Resort. I looked like a floating Amber Alert, with a light-up, two-foot margarita in my hand. As groups of happy families floated past me, I tried to engage them in conversation.

"Hi!! Fun pool! Where are you guys from?"

The moms would just glare at me and hurry their children out of my reach. I may as well have been shouting, "What a beautiful child! She's the perfect size to fit in the trunk of my car!"

At least I was outside. I floated around and around. Alone.

With a week to go, I hung in my hotel room for a few days. I had to get my act together to actually film at the end of the week. I couldn't show up to set as I was—an unhinged loner. I started to work on my part. I was playing a girl named Betty.

The reports I would get about Billy every morning from the production assistant were escalating. Apparently, Billy was so out of control with partying and strippers that the movie studio had actually placed him under a curfew, a sort of Vegas "house arrest." Billy was not allowed to leave his hotel room after nine at night (unless we were shooting) lest the movie not get finished.

The night before I was finally supposed to shoot, the rest of the cast and crew had been bonding and had planned a group outing to see the Cirque Du Soleil's *O*. I was not invited. Everyone was going to see *O* but me and Billy.

I received a call from Billy's assistant, Lisa.

"Billy wants to have a meeting with you tonight."

Shit!

"Isn't this something we can talk about on the set in the morning?"

"Billy really wants to see you . . . and he hates to be alone."

Now?!? After three weeks, Billy wants to see me *now*? I knew that meant I was being summoned to his hotel room, and it was already 10 p.m. Terror welled up inside me, and I (correctly) felt like I was being fed to the lions. I pleaded with Lisa.

"I don't know. I haven't had dinner yet . . . maybe we could meet for a bite to eat?"

"He's not allowed out of his room."

"Um . . . "

I heard some mumbling in the background.

"Billy says he'll buy you a grilled cheese."

Now I *love* me some grilled cheese, but my gut had alarm bells going off. Even though this was the director of my first big movie, no part of me wanted to be alone in a hotel with him. Nevertheless, I didn't know how to get out of it.

"Okay. I guess so. Give me twenty."

Even the offer of grilled cheese wasn't enough to calm down my nerves. The next twenty minutes were spent calling everyone I knew asking advice on how to handle it.

"He's your director—he just wants to talk. What's the big deal?"

I had every reason to be on high alert. Each morning's call to put me "on hold" had provided me with the running saga of Billy. Billy had a girlfriend who lived in New York. Everyone on the set knew that he was having parties with hookers and strippers late at night in his hotel room. There was even a special person hired, who was essentially a "hooker wrangler." (It made me sad to think that even the hooker wrangler had bonded with the cast and crew and I had not.)

The mornings that Billy's girlfriend would fly in for a set visit, the hooker wrangler went into high gear. She would have to clear out all the naked ladies, bottles of booze, coke, and any other illicit evidence from the room. Just as the last G-string was swept out of his hotel room, Billy was propped up with a Red Bull, thrown in the shower, handed a fresh pair of leather pants, and was ready to greet his lucky lady with open arms.

I was out of my cool league in a major way. As you know, up until that point, my acting career had mostly consisted of me playing characters who were TV unfuckable.

As I walked down the corridor to Billy's hotel room, it was new territory for me. I knew how to talk to men in Batman shirts, not hooker lovers in leather pants. The fact that I was in the movie at all felt like a bit of a miracle. I knocked on his door, praying to God.

"Dear Lord, please let this be a real meeting, peer to peer, employer to employee, . . . and let the grilled cheese be there already."

No such luck. Billy opened the door shirtless, buzzed, and groggy.

Oh nooooooooooooooooooo.

The room was pitch-black, and Billy looked like I had woken him up from being passed out or caught in the middle of another bender. I can only imagine what the woman on hooker cleanup patrol had to deal with.

"Oh, heeeeyyyyyyy . . . yeah, you . . . "

Did he forget that he'd summoned me?

"Yeah, Lisa said you wanted to talk to me about Betty?"

"Riiiiiiggghhht, yeah, come in."

Billy flipped on a lamp to reveal a room that looked like it had been trashed by Keith Moon in his heyday. Every surface was covered in ashtrays, clothes, cigarettes, empty bottles of Jim Beam, and bongs.

I panicked and summoned my best impression of my mother. When in doubt—compliment!

"I love your room . . . it's really . . . festive."

"Whatever."

He did not put on a shirt. He did light up a smoke. More important, there was no grilled cheese in sight. Bastard! Of course, this fucker didn't eat solid food. It would combat all the coke and Beam he was ingesting. What kind of sick sociopath was I dealing with who would promise a girl grilled cheese and then not deliver?

I scanned the room for somewhere to sit that was not on his gigantic bed that really just looked like a gigantic sex platform—a sex platform that I was not up to (and lacked the technical skills) to perform on. Billy was three years younger than me, but he scared the living daylights out of me. My eyes landed on a piece of art on his bureau—it was about a foot and a half tall, all white, and was an incredibly detailed sculpture of a man with a huge boner penetrating a woman from behind—doggy style. *Run, Arden, run!!!!*

Why didn't I just leave? Why did I stay? I can only speak for myself. This woman didn't know how to leave. I was stunned, and I was afraid. I didn't know how to get out of there in a manner that kept my job. My defense mechanism was to keep it nice and polite, as I am sure so many other women have had to do over the years. I was afraid that if I left, I would get fired, or that Billy would have thought I was overreacting or just being uptight. I was afraid that he would call my agents and tell people that I was "difficult," or worse, that I was "unprofessional."

I hadn't booked many movies before, so this was a big deal to me, and I just wanted to be able to do my job without having to worry about being sent to my boss's hotel room. Not to mention the fact that I want to believe everyone is inherently good and that a guy wouldn't deliberately put me in a situation that would upset me/disgust me/et cetera.

Of course, I know that's not true, but I wanted to believe it, especially because I know so many good men who would never belittle me like this. So who are all these others who think this is appropriate behavior? I didn't know what to do. So I did what I was trained to do—what my mom had to do when *she* was chased around her desk by her boss when she was twenty-two. I summoned my best JJ Myrin and started complimenting the décor.

"Wow! Did that come with your room? I don't have any art in mine."

Run, Arden, run!!!!

"Oh, that? I don't know . . . Have a seat."

Oh my god.

Billy gestured to his sex platform. No way, buddy. All I knew was I could not get on that bed. But I still wanted to be polite. Why couldn't I tell him to fuck off?

"Wow! You have a sitting area! How cool . . . I don't have a settee. Lucky you."

"Huh?"

Even Eagle Hat hadn't looked at me like I was such a total loser. I nervously crossed over and perched on the edge of an ugly foam chair in his "seating area."

"What a cool armchair. I wonder if they got this at Design Within Reach? I love that store."

"Take off your skirt."

Huh?! Wow—he really cut to the chase. Clearly, he had done this before. And I am guessing some terrified young ladies had agreed.

"No, thank you. Sooooo . . . Lisa said you wanted to talk to me about my character, Betty?"

"Betty's a fucking joke."

Not only did he not respect me as a woman, but now he was degrading the part I was so proud to have booked.

"Take off your skirt."

"I'm not going to take off my skirt."

After an awkward pause, I continued. "This settee really makes the room much more livable. It seems like you have really settled in here."

Points for poise. I started to have an out-of-body experience and couldn't believe I was having my own *Hurlyburly*[23] Hollywood moment. I had never experienced anything close to the casting couch before. I didn't think it would be so on the nose. This was crazy. I felt so sorry and angry for all the women who this happened to on a regular basis. I am so lucky he didn't actually lurch at me. Did I stand up for myself? No. I did what I always did. I stalled and changed the subject.

"Where's the grilled cheese, Billy?"

"If I order grilled cheese, will you take off your skirt?"

This fucker played dirty.

"Just take off your skirt."

"You know what? I need to go. I have to go learn my lines for tomorrow."

Technically, I had about eight words in the whole movie. If I had not already learned them in three and a half weeks, something would have been seriously wrong with me. But that was beside the point, and I wanted to seem professional. Clearly, Billy didn't give two shits if I thought he was professional or not, but I still wanted him to like me. Sadly, the need to please runs deep.

Before I could even think about it, I made a quick exit and immediately called all my funny friends in Batman shirts, and we laughed our asses off about what a total tool Billy was. I tried to make light of it, to make it a funny story, a cocktail party anecdote. I didn't allow myself to be angry—to see how degrading and inappropriate and dangerous and diminishing it

---

23. *Hurlyburly* is a David Rabe play and movie about Hollywood execs and a casting director who treat women like a tradeable commodity.

all was. I didn't know how to own my anger over the fact that I was put in that position in the first place.

So instead, I did what I knew how to do—make a joke out of it. Laugh it off. I guess on some level I didn't think anyone would care, and I'd be pegged as uptight if I was upset about it. This makes me sad for my younger self. I wish she knew she had value. The next day on the set, we were shooting at the good old Circus-Circus Hotel—my old stomping grounds. Billy approached me as I stood in line to get a waffle.

"Pretty crazy night last night, huh?"

"Yeah. Pretty crazy."

The hooker wrangler shot me a look. Did she think I had humped Leather Pants?

I hate to admit it, but I didn't say anything or go to HR, because he was my boss. I wanted to keep my job. I wanted to be liked. I didn't want to offend him. I didn't know it was okay to have a problem with things that are clearly not okay. I didn't know I could have my own back.

So to that young lady who was panicked and nervous and making weird jokes in that hotel room in Vegas so many years ago: You did the best you could. You got out. And it *is* okay to tell HR and let people deal with the consequences of their own actions. Even now it feels scary. But it is even scarier not to say anything at all—to shove it down and plant a seed of shame inside yourself that grows and grows.

Billy Leather Pants—I wanted to leave, I just wanted to do my job, and the way you treated me was not okay. Just because you were bored and sequestered to your room, my self-esteem and my body are not something to be used as a toy, or a plaything, or a distraction—something to entertain you and then degrade and toss away. I hope you never treated another woman like that again. But I am afraid there is a good chance that you probably did,

*

Two Broads Abroad

Travel broadens the horizons! Exposure to foreign lands offers us an opportunity to soak up the native customs of different cultures and bring some of what we learned back to our own dusty lives at home. Living three thousand miles away from my mom, I really tried to go out of my way to go on some fun adventures with her. She was so sparkly and bright and ready for anything. Since I couldn't see JJ day to day, I went for quality not quantity in our outings.

I took her to a drag show in NYC, on a beach getaway in Hawaii, to a cattle ranch Thanksgiving in the mountains of Los Olivios, and to see Bruno Mars for her seventy-fifth birthday at Madison Square Garden. I did this because I loved her, but more important, I kind of owed her. BIG TIME. You see, when I graduated from college, JJ took me on a surprise mother–daughter ten-day getaway around England and France (and I am pretty sure I tortured her).

Ah, Jolly Old England! Land of history and castles and fancy accents! I had never been out of the country before and was eager to soak in all the culture and sights. Turns out I am a very specific traveler. In England, I only wanted to go to attractions that were haunted.

I dragged JJ on a ghost tour of the creepiest sites in England, convinced I was an oracle after a very cryptic Ouija board game with my friend Leah in college. I had a very pressing question I was asking the spirit world (whether I should cut my bangs or not) when the heart-shaped plastic ghost game piece thingy suddenly started going crazy of its own accord, spelling out messages about death and murder, and subsequently flew off the board. You don't have to tell me twice, Satan! Leah and I ran screaming from the basement, donating our game board to the demons that lived in her boiler room.

Needless to say, I was excited about my new status as the Gateway to the Portal to Hell and was anxious to explore my connection to the underworld. The Tower of England was the first stop on our mother–daughter bonding tour. You could just feel centuries of bad vibes wanting to kill you. Maybe the ghost of Anne Boleyn had a message she wanted to give me to tell the world? I dragged my mom from cell to cell at the Tower, trying to find Anne's ghost.

"Anne Boleyn. If you can hear me, my name is Arden, I come from Little Compton, Rhode Island, and I am happy to spread any voodoo messages for you from the underworld!"

Nothing. Her ghost was ghosting me. The only contact I had with Anne Boleyn was with the nifty *Other Boleyn Girl* guillotine souvenir I bought at the gift shop. That sucker would pass through fingers but slice cigarettes with precision. As my mom and I toured the countryside, I would scour gift shops looking for regional ghost books for the local area. JJ just wanted to see gardens that were in full bloom, and instead I dragged her to dungeons where people had been tortured or left to starve and die. Mother–daughter bonding at its finest! Janet and I were having a great time. I definitely was.

Our next stop on our tour—Paris! En route, I was forced to face my claustrophobia fears when Janet dragged me on the Chunnel between London and France. Halfway through the trip under the English Channel I started to freak out (see: submarine visit with Cub Scouts, page 8), and my mother had to ply me with booze. I arrived in France tipsy and gasping for air. "Bonjour, France! Je suis arrived!" Everyone was so French and elegant. I was a little out of my league.

In school, whenever I would take a crack at speaking French, my inability to concentrate or wrap my tongue around that pesky romance language left my persnickety French teacher, Mr. Buckley, plugging his ears and yelling, "*Non! Non! Non!*"

"*Ou est la valise, Sylvie? La valise est on the table, Phillippe.*"

"*Non!* Arden, *non!!!! Arrêtez! Arrêtez!!*"

It physically hurt Mr. Buckley to hear me speak French. He agreed to pass me if *I agreed* to never take French again. Sounded fair to me. Before Janet and I headed off to France, I wanted to show her that my education was not a total waste. She wanted to use a travel agent, but I insisted on setting up our whole trip for us.

"I got this, Mom. It will be *très magnifique*! Paris, boutique hotels, croissants. Ooh la la!"

We arrived in France to discover that I had smugly booked all the hotels for the wrong month. I became extremely embarrassed, panicked, and refused to speak in French for the rest of the two-week trip. My mother had never taken French in her life and was left to fend for the two of us.

"*Ma petit daughter, n'est pas le number une person qui parle le française.*"

Our terrible linguistic skills didn't matter. Turns out that the French speak English anyway. I win again, Mssr. Buckley! I told you I didn't need to learn it! *Qui est le dumb-dumb maintenent? Pas moi!* (I was also not the one with a bad comb-over, a permanently stuffed-up nose, and living with my mother at the age of fifty.)

When my mom and I traveled, we really liked to cut to the chase and hit the most important things on a trip. Why go tour a big, boring museum when you can go right to a museum gift shop? How much better can the original *Mona Lisa* painting be than the reproduction of her mysterious eyes on a souvenir Mona Lisa bobblehead? Sold! I didn't have to hoof it all over a big stuffy museum to get to da Vinci's money shot. Jokes on you, Louvre!

After hitting the gift shops at the *Musées* Louvre and Rodin and stuffing our faces with crêpes for breakfast, lunch, and dinner for a week, my mom and I were exhausted. We needed a day in the country to refresh ourselves.

Janet and I decided to take a day trip out to the most French of all French tourist attractions in the beautiful countryside— Euro Disney. I guess we could have gone to Versailles, come to think of it. I mean, it's *a little* more historical. But WHY GO ANYWHERE when you can go to Euro Disney?! Like a magical, deserted work of art, Euro Disney made us feel like we were in Orlando, but the apocalypse had come and we were the last people on earth. *Vive la France!* Being at Euro Disney was like seeing a real live European dinosaur.

It was strange to approach an almost deserted Thunder Mountain and see super skinny French guys dressed up as cowboys from the Wild West. These were definitely cowboys who rolled their own clove cigarettes and talked about existentialism in their off time. These French cowboys had to stand guard at their western trading post with bandanas covering their faces like banditos, wearing ten-gallon hats and replica pistols that weighed down their holsters and appeared to be too heavy for the cowboys.

As we approached, *le Banditos en Français* looked at us with disdain and lazily twirled their pistols.

"Get in your corrals and wait your turn. O-chay?"

"O-chay," my mom replied, giggling. (To be fair, Mr. Buckley laughed at my French for years, so we were just getting even.) I wasn't sure why we were being corralled, as no one else was in line. We were momentarily distracted from the world's most judgmental cowboys when a gaggle of French moms arrived behind us and pushed their kids to cut in front of us in the line. *No one else was at Euro Disney*, but those moms had to shove their kids onto Thunder Mountain before us. You go ladies—bring up that *bébé*!

Having returned to US soil with so much culture under my belt, I felt like a changed woman. I was worldly and *très* sophisticated. To celebrate our official post-collegiate entry into adulthood, Sheryle and I decided to head out for an evening in Newport, Rhode Island, home of the fancy mansions. We wanted to announce our place in society as fine young ladies, the same way all nice young ladies do—with an evening of drunken karaoke in a Merchant Marine bar.

Sheryle and I hit the town with my brother and his friend Andrew. Unlike me and Alarik, Andrew had been raised with very proper manners. (Not that Janet didn't try. She did. We are just monsters.) Andrew knows which fork to use and has dimples the size of craters on his cheeks.

Our classy journey got kicked off with a few gin and tonics and a very elegant rendition of "If You Want My Body." (I was proud of myself for edging away from my usual trashy cocktail, the Sea Breeze.) Alarik had decided to go out for the night "draped in linen" like a sailboat, and I wore my most elegant outfit, a floor-length silver Contempo Casuals skirt and a mandarin see-through beaded blouse. I looked like a Stevie Nicks robot.

Two gin and tonics in and I quickly advanced to my karaoke ace in the hole, "I like Big Butts (Baby Got Back)," by Sir-Mix-A-Lot. As I was shaking my silver booty in the window for all the passersby to see, Sheryle noticed our fanciest friend from college strolling outside, Chase Nightingale.

Chase had grown up in Manhattan but spent summers in one of the historic mansions that the rest of us plebeians had to pay admission fees to enter. Sheryle darted out the door and chased him down.

"Chase! Chase! Want to come have a dance-off?"

Chase was not nibbling at her fabulous offer. Attempting to shake us off, he muttered something about a house party his buddy Tyler was having, that he had to go to, and casually tossed off the address to us if we wanted to "swing by." I'm guessing he assumed we would never show up.

"We'll be there! Yes! We're *in*!!!"

And swing by we did! After polishing off a few more gin and tonics and the remains of the karaoke Color Me Badd song book (I Wanna to Sex *You* Up, Newport!), we were en route to Tyler's house. The four of us mobilized, and I laid down our plan of attack:

Blend in.

Seem fancy.

Don't embarrass Chase.

As we approached Tyler's house, we realized our dreams were coming true—we were at one of the real tycoon mansions. It was extra exciting because this family was so rich they didn't even need the tax write-off of hosting tours—they had this palace all to themselves. We would be some of the first common folk to set foot in its gilded halls. But we were ready! I took the lead in my elegant silver outfit.

"Okay, everybody. Be cool. If we blend in and act like we belong, no one will even take notice of us."

With our marching orders in place, we stormed the castle. We approached the door, I rang the bell, and Andrew stepped in a huge pile of dog shit. He panicked, and not knowing what to do with the offending pile, he took a tissue from his pocket and removed the shit from his shoe just as the door swung open. A forty-five-year-old man in yacht wear stood before us.

"Can I help you?"

"Yes, we're friends with Chase Nightingale."

"Yes?"

"We're supposed to meet him here."

"Oh, okay . . . um . . . please come in."

Our host seemed baffled but ushered us inside. As we entered the marble foyer, Andrew had nowhere to put the dog shit, so he held a tissue in his hand hoping to quickly find a garbage can. We all entered the residence of the former robber baron: Robot Stevie Nicks, Draped in Linen Alarik, slightly buzzed Sheryle, and Andrew with a hostess gift of a fresh dog turd. When arriving at a party, it is always important to come bearing a hostess gift.

Chase had not arrived, and it quickly became clear that everyone was older than us by a good twenty years. These apparently were the parents of the people who were throwing the party later. Most of them were older, married, and had a shade of pink that comes with having loads of money and spending many days of leisure on a yacht or tennis court. One man was actually wearing an ascot. For real. And not in a costume party kind of way; ascots were just his jam.

We were early. Like *two hours* early. Our friend was nowhere to be seen, so essentially we were a group of strangers crashing a dinner party at a mansion, one carrying a tissue filled with dog shit in his hand.

The four of us decided to divide and conquer. We made our way into the party of elder statesmen where we tried to mix in with people with names like Topper, Cricket, Hunter, and Wesley. I headed straight for the bar, where I tried to fit in, ordering another breezy gin and tonic. My host pulled out a huge tumbler-size glass and started pouring.

"We're out of tonic."

"That is *not* a problem!"

The biggest lightweight in all the land got handed a sophisticated gin and tonic that was basically just a tumbler full of gin. Bottoms up!

I was enjoying my drink and more and more *really* enjoying my own company. I started to feel like I could totally fit right in with Buffy and Kimber and Kip. I complimented them on their fancy watches and their deep-sea tans.

"Great look! Shorts at night with cashmere on top? I love it—you've got seasons coming and going!"

"How do you know the hosts?"

"You know . . . just *Newport*. Isn't everyone connected through someone else? Who can keep track?"

"Uh-huh."

"Does this house have a dumbwaiter?"

I laughed a little too loud. I told them I lived on a ranch in Little Compton. I declined to say that it was a ranch *house*.

My gin and tonic without the tonic was really loosening me up. I had finally found my people, and it turns out my people have their initials embroidered on their shirts and wear man scarves. Who cares that Chase never showed up to vouch for us and we basically crashed Thurston Howell III's house? Now that kitty cat had her drink on, it was time to get her flirt on.

Alarik, Sheryle, Andrew, and the dog shit were nowhere in sight. No matter. I was becoming more and more charming with each gulp of my new favorite drink. Since there were no guys even close to my age, I decided to try out my gin-soaked charms on a nice older architect named Charles who was standing in the butler's pantry. It appeared Charles may have been standing with his age-appropriate and elegant wife, but I did not let that deter me. I needed to flirt, and flirt I did.

Charles and I started to chat. But rather than just wow him with my American twenty-one-year-old self, I decided to bump it up a notch. That's right. I became the douche who went to England for ten days and came back with a *fake British accent*.

"Where do you live, Arden?"

"Oh me? Well my mate and I just took this flat in New York. It's on the third floor but at least there is a lift."

"I'm sorry, where are you from?"

"Little Compton, but I was just on holiday back in the old country. This party is brilliant!"

"Uh-huh. So, you're moving to New York?"

"Aren't you a cheeky lad, Charles! You must ring me if you are ever in the city."

Sheryle rounded the bend, having just returned from helping Andrew discreetly store the dog shit in a planter outside the Gatsby mansion. She was greeted by me close talking Charles with this winner: "I smashed my hand in a door but they took me to hospital, so all was well. I had a silver fingernail sewn on, love."

Sheryle quickly realized what was happening, that her best friend was attempting to use the world's worst British accent to try to hit on a middle-aged married dad architect. Sheryle claims that in that moment time stood still, *Matrix* style. Her friend was in trouble. Big trouble.

"Oh, you like my frock? Cheers!"

"Nooooo!!!!!!!!!!!!!!!!!!"

Sheryle slowly shoved everyone out of the way and dove in like a hostage rescuer to carry me out of there.

"Hey, Arden, it's time to go."

"What? No, Charles was just telling me about his brother the barrister."

"I'm sorry for my friend. She is troubled."

I had never been forcibly removed by my scruff before, and I didn't like it.

"Cock blockers! I think he is really into me!" I slurred as they threw me in the back seat of JJ's old Camry station wagon and sped away.

As we rounded Ocean Avenue we cruised right in front of the International Tennis Hall of Fame. Home of grass courts, elegance, white clothes, and etiquette for over a century.

"Stop the car! Stop the car!!! I need to get out tout suite!"

I barrel rolled out of the stopped car and weaved my way up to take a gander at the trophies in the window. Pressing my nose against the glass, I peered in at the emblems of generations of good breeding and success.

"Fancy Nancys live here. I'm so fancy! I play tennis on lawns! I win trophies! Hey, assholes, look at my trophy case!"

Circling under the awning for a few moments, I finally came in for my landing. I stood on the sidewalk in my robot outfit, sprayed the outside of the International Tennis Hall of Fame with vomit, and then curled up like a little silver ball on the sidewalk to take a nice snooze. My work was done there.

My brother was appalled, and Andrew and Sheryle were bored. I begged my friends to go on without me.

"I'm sure Charles will come looking for me soon enough."

"Get up."

"You are all just jealous that he was chatting *me* up."

"Come on. Let's go home."

It took us six hours to make the forty-five-minute drive home. I vomited my way from the Tennis Museum to historical cemeteries to fields with cows in them. When we finally got home, I was drunk for two more days. I think I sweated gin until mid-August. I was *disgusted* with myself and was waiting for JJ to bring down the hammer. She never did.

"I'm just happy you dragged your brother out and had fun for the night. I can't believe *my kids* were in the Nightingale mansion. Tell. Me. EVERYTHING. Did they have fancy towels in the bathroom? I bet they had fancy towels."

"Oh, they weren't just fancy . . . they were *monogrammed*."

"Ooooooooooh, I knew it!!!!!"

Grief Island

Most people don't want to spend much time thinking about death. But the sad fact is, no one gets a free pass, and in my experience, everyone goes a little bonkers around it. My father Willy passed away in the summer of 2017. He was so sick for so many years of my life that I thought I could pre-grieve him.

Willy was a complicated person—not the warmest or healthiest guy, plus he lived life *hard*. Lots of booze, cigarettes, cakes, and butter. His brazenly unhealthy lifestyle was nipping at his heels for decades. At least a dozen times over the years, I was told my father was going to die. Each time I would have to go say goodbye to him, he would miraculously rebound. It was a very strange thing, like the boy who cried wolf.

On the one hand, it was always a happy miracle that he had survived, but it was also exhausting to gear up for a death and then have it not happen. Add to that the fact that, growing up, I always had to sort of keep his brushes with death a secret. I think my mom was embarrassed that my dad had such a struggle with alcohol: we just never talked about it. Early on I learned to just zip my lip.

Starting at age eleven, I would stuff down each of my dad's close calls as if they didn't matter and I shouldn't bother people with them. It felt like I was always holding my breath, bracing for a crash landing, waiting for the phone call that Willy had actually passed away. I would quietly feel sad about my dying father, but I maintained an upbeat, funny presence at school. Thirty-two years of held breath, thirty-two years of faking upbeat ease while having a dying father. I thought maybe if I grieved in advance, I could get a free pass when he actually died.

Sadly, that was not my experience at all. When my father finally passed away, it was incredibly painful, partly because we were not close, and partly because it was brutal toward the end to see this intimidating figure shrinking before my eyes. He almost looked like a baby swaddled in a Patriots sweat suit. I wish I could say that my father and I had this big come-to-Jesus conversation where everything that was not said to each other was finally said—but that was not how it went down for us, and that's okay. My father died as he lived—brash and distant. Despite everything, I told him "I love you" the last time I saw him. He did say, "Love you, too." That was the only time he ever said it.

What if I told you what I was most afraid of? What if I told you that I'd always felt so damaged and so unlovable because I suspected that my father never loved me or even really liked me? It is hard to believe a parent could dislike their offspring, but it happens. He would say things like, "Who would want to marry you?" When Dan called Willy to tell him that he loved me and that he wanted to ask permission to spend the rest of his life with me, all Willy said was "Good luck" and passed the phone to my mom.

For many years I felt like a chair with one broken leg—I'd won the lottery with a glorious mother; a wonderful, hilarious brother (even though we teased each other often, Alarik Myrin is the funniest, kindest, smartest bro I could ask for, and I would not be who I am without him); and amazing friends.

Eventually I learned that I don't have to be a broken four-legged chair. Instead, I can be a gorgeous, spectacular, perfectly formed three-legged stool. Complete as is. Everyone gets dealt a certain hand in life—some people just can't give love. I think my father was one of those people. But ever so slowly I have learned that not only am I enough, but there is the possibility that I have *always* been enough—I just didn't know it because my father told me otherwise.

When Willy died, I mourned him and what we never had. With grief, the only way to the other side is just to put on your big-girl pants and walk through that murky fire. However, there was a certain beauty and magic to the year after his passing. I was basically out of my mind; there was so much adrenaline and a flurry of feelings flooding my system, but instinctively I knew how to set up my own path to heal. I called it Grief Island. I'd like to share everything I learned from my first go-round on Grief Island and its magical healing powers.

While no one is fully prepared to grieve, it's okay to do it your own way, even with a little flair and panache. And to anyone who has a friend who is grieving, it's okay to text your condolences. I used to think that if I texted someone my sympathies, it felt cold or like I was bothering them. I thought I needed to write a proper condolence card, and if I didn't, I felt like I had to hide from them in shame.

The reality is that loads of people reached out to me via text when my father passed, and each one of the texts touched me and helped heal some small part of myself. It meant something to me that people were thinking about what I was going through.

Do what you gotta do, honey! Don't judge your angels. When grieving, you're a lunatic—at least I was. On Grief Island, I pictured myself like a badass warrior, looking somewhat like the musician IZ—gentle yet fierce, graceful yet steady.

Immediately I moved to Atlanta for five months to shoot season one of *Insatiable*, the Netflix show I'm on. So I packed up and headed off to Grief Island: The Atlanta Airbnb Edition. I made up rules for myself; the first month I cancelled anything I didn't want to do. I needed to show up for work and do the bare minimum so I could make some cash, so I didn't get evicted, but beyond that I really lowered the bar.

Little did I know that my Florence Nightingale–style grief counselor would come in the form of reality TV. Don't fight the healing powers of reality TV! Reality TV nursed me back to life—specifically *The Great British Bake Off* (i.e., the TV equivalent of Prozac). I watched three seasons of this heavenly show in six days. The angel that is Mary Berry[24] and her piercing blue eyes made me feel like everything was going to be okay each time she called something "scrummy."

Mary's eyes are balanced out by Paul Hollywood's creepy tans and odd flirting with the young contestants. All the contestants are so kind to one another, and the only prizes at stake are a large plate, a bouquet of flowers, and the title of Britain's best amateur baker. I have always found it hard to cry in real life, but suddenly I became incredibly sentimental watching Paul the prison guard (with the never-mentioned scar on his face that I like to think was the result of a prison knife fight) bake a gorgeous, giant lion constructed entirely out of dinner rolls; it made me weep like a baby.

I would go into deep dives online about the contestants— young Martha became a superstar and Ruby ended up shaving

---

24. I also really love the new judge, Prue Leith, and her cornucopia of eyeglasses.

her head and publicly bashing Paul Hollywood. Googling these amateur bakers soothed me as my mind and heart were processing the loss of my father.

As Mary Berry initially helped put this Humpty Dumpty back together again, another area of reality TV kept me connected to the outside world—*The Bachelor* franchise. I host the world's silliest podcast, called *Will You Accept This Rose?*, in which I discuss the show with fellow comedians who also happen to be *Bachelor* superfans. While I was on Grief Island for my dad, my podcast was the one thing I wouldn't miss. Watching young bodybuilders, dental hygienists, and "content creators" fall in love and discussing it with my funny friends was about all the focus my brain could handle.

How did Robby make his hair swoop like that? Who would have thought Raven and Adam would end up together? How much money does Chris Harrison make? Can I have his job? How would I do as a contestant in the mansion?

Doing my podcast with my merry band of cohorts filled (and continues to fill) my heart. I never really played group sports, but all of a sudden I had built this team of funny oddballs who care about and obsessively follow the exploits of insanely attractive and hairless people looking for love. Hearing *Criminal Minds* star Paget Brewster offer conspiracy theories—like the one that ABC offered Dean's dad a few acres of land in exchange for being rude to Dean and Rachel during Hometown Visits Week—is all I needed in my life. It is so surprising to me that a podcast about *The Bachelor* franchise has become a huge part of my life, brought me all sorts of new friends, and ended up being the best grief therapy a gal could ask for.

The podcast was also healing for my mom, who accidentally became a star on the podcast. As my dad was in the final few months of his life, JJ called in one day during an episode. When we started recording the episode, I forgot to turn my phone to airplane mode, so my phone rang through to the studio and was plugged in to our audio equipment. Suddenly my phone conversation with my mom was recording.

"Ohmygod! Arden. There's a cat hoarder! He's on the news!"

"Mom, I'm doing the podcast right now. I can't talk."

This was never a deterrent to JJ when she needed to chat.

"This freak just surrendered seventy-six cats to the shelters all over Massachusetts. Lori and I are on our way right now. Seventy-six cats! What a freak show!"

My mom went on and on and was all hyped up and ready to get her paws on a cat. My producers, Katie and Anna, ended up leaving her phone call in the edit of the episode that we posted. I didn't think much of it, until people started e-mailing us saying how much they loved my mom and wanted to hear about what happened with her and the cats. Well, my mom did adopt one of those cats. She was the runt of the litter—a tiny tuxedo cat with giant paws and two sets of "thumbs." She named her Mittens.

Mittens the kitten—look at those paws!

Little did I know that hosting a *Bachelor* podcast would also become a huge part of my mom's grief therapy. She started watching *The Bachelor*, too, and calling in to the podcast more and more as my dad was getting sicker. Whenever anyone on the podcast would talk about my mom, they always used her full podcast title: Janet Myrin of Little Compton Real Estate, "for all your summer rental needs." My mom would call in with theories on who was going to win the final rose on the show and who she had a crush on; or on off weeks, give us hot real estate tips for Little Compton.

"I've got a great house with a barn that has to move *fast* because this guy needs to move back to Italy. If you act now, you can get it for under $600,000. Oh, and Ari is a horny creep."

"That Rachel is the best Bachelorette they ever had. Why did she pick Bryan? I don't trust a mama's boy with cheek implants."

"Colton is so gay. It would be so much more interesting if they had twelve guys *and* twelve gals competing for him. Now *that's* a show I would like. Also, I've got two acres of waterfront land that finally passed its septic test that's about to go on the market."

My podcast and *The Bachelor* franchise connected me and my mom more and more and was a nice, seemingly frivolous but actually very healing, distraction from watching my father fading away.

Two weeks after my father died I did a live podcast at the Outside Lands Music and Arts Festival with five of *The Bachelor*'s contestants and got to walk around the woods flanked by five of the hottest guys on earth. I have to say, *Bachelor* and *Bachelorette* contestants are *far better looking* than any other humans I have ever met. That includes movie stars. These guys were my hunky TV grief angels. My friend and fellow comedian

With Dean—one of my TV grief angels.

Guy Branum was so struck by how handsome all the *Bachelorette* contestants were that he kept talking to them and saying that of course they are handsome: they are HUMAN PRIZES.

I even got to sing a song with a band. I did Journey's "Don't Stop Believin'," and I did a stage dive into the loving arms of Alex the bachelor, who is also a hot Russian accountant. Finally, I was starting to feel joyful again— crazy but joyful, and reality TV was a big part of that. I wanted to share this feeling with my family.

My mom's favorite TV show was *Project Runway*. I had just done the pilot of *Insatiable* with Alyssa Milano (who at that point I really didn't know very well, but I knew she hosted *Project Runway All Stars*). This sweet human hooked my mom and me up with tickets to the finale of *Project Runway All Stars* the day after my father's funeral.

My mom wore her best QVC Isaac Mizrahi jacket to meet Isaac, and she requested a makeover and fake eyelashes. I got her all ready and off we went, where she got to take a photo *with* Isaac *in* her Isaac. JJ loved her Willy Myrin. That bad boy in the office who dared her to marry him all fifty years prior. But at *Project Runway* she shined even though she was hurting. And once again, reality TV healed me and my family.

Mama Myrin in her Isaac Mizrahi, meeting Isaac Mizrahi.

When my father did pass away, we had him cremated. We were shown a variety of urns at the funeral parlor, each more formal than the last. None of them felt like him or like we were doing right by who he was. At last we realized we had to bury him in his one true love—his security blanket, his safe place—his soda cooler, the only relationship he did not enter into on a dare. I also tried to include a photo of Heather Locklear from *T. J. Hooker* with him, but Alarik put his foot down. Drip.

So, You Accidentally Kicked America's Sweetheart in the Face?

When you grow up in a farm town with more cows than people, the idea of getting to be on television someday seems as likely as being able to fly. Killing time at the general store doesn't exactly prepare you for how to keep your cool on a movie set. One of the strange things about being a huge television and movie aficionado and actually getting to be an actor for a living is that there is a big difference between the *thrill* of booking a job and then the *terror* of having to actually go execute it. I have a deadly combination of social anxiety coupled with being a pop culture superfan—not exactly the perfect mix for an actor to show up and be calm and cool when working with an idol.

Most working actors in LA pay the bills by performing a medley of guest spots on episodic television, commercials, and voiceovers in between waiting for their big break. When I book guest spots on popular TV shows, it's a balancing act of having to keep my shit together and appear professional over the course of a week or month, while deep down I am freaking out over the fact that I am face to face with people I have watched on television for years. It's like being a guest at someone else's family dinner, except everyone in the family is famous.

Over the years I have spent a week or two on many TV shows, often playing very peculiar characters. I have been the wacky neighbor, the uptight wedding coordinator, Corbin Bernsen's super tan stalker, Jeremy Sisto's super lonely stalker, half of a Christian couple that swings, a horny bank teller, a weepy mistress, a murderous hand model/mini golf champ, and first runner-up Miss Nude Reno, among others. Even my first real onscreen romantic kiss was unusual; for many years I only got comedy kisses—that is, kisses in *MADtv* sketches with me and Bobby Lee wearing odd man wigs. (Everyone on *MADtv* had to make out with one another in sketches, typically while wearing a fat suit, a bad wig, or covered in fake blood.)

When I booked my first real onscreen romantic kiss, I was so nervous. I wanted to appear professional and calm, only to realize that comedians aren't the only odd ducks when it comes to staged romance. The actor whom I booked a romantic scene with had a pre-show exercise before our love scene that included barking like a dog, eating egg salad, doing fifteen pushups, and smoking a cigar right before we made out. Wow. Even Flight Frenzy did not taste like egg salad and cigar. Truth be told, dog impressions are still way better than dog shit.

But it wasn't until I was booked on an episode of *Friends* that I really felt like I had arrived! I had been a fan of the show for many years, so it was incredibly bizarre to be on the set in Monica and Chandler's living room. It felt like all my childhood dreams had come true, and I actually got to move *into* my television. Oh my god—there's Central Perk!!!! One grande latte for me, Gunther!!

My episode was during their eighth season, which meant I was probably their 1,500th guest star, and as such, I had very low expectations of chatting with any of the stars of the show. When you add in the fact that the other guest star for the week was Sean Penn, I really felt insecure, like the freshman in high school who had snuck into the cool seniors' party—but I didn't care! I was in MONICA'S APARTMENT!

The week was extra unusual because it was right after 9/11, and there were threats around Hollywood. At the beginning of the week, the people who ran the Warner Brothers lot held a safety meeting informing everyone how to evacuate in case anyone found anthrax in the studio. Never did I think I'd be doing an anthrax drill with Jeff Spicoli and Ross Geller!

The part I was playing was Brenda the maid. Brenda's a woman whom Monica and Chandler hired to clean their apartment. The storyline revolved around the fact that Brenda is threatening to Monica because Monica is such a neat freak: she doesn't want anyone else to clean her space. Monica is convinced that Brenda stole her favorite jeans, which happen to have an ink spot on the crotch, and the only way to prove it is for Monica to get a glimpse of Brenda's crotch. Everything culminated in a scene in which I had to climb all over the kitchen counter and Courteney Cox had to try to look at my snooch. It was a fun Lucy and Ethel moment that hinged on physical comedy.

By the eighth season, the cast was a well-oiled machine—I think we rehearsed twice. I have never been great with props, and this entire part required a dozen items that I had to maneuver around the set, like ladders and buckets, feather dusters and brooms. I would have naturally been awkward with all that stuff anyway, but in another environment I would have just gone and practiced on the set until I felt confident that I could do the scene smoothly. However, there was no way in hell I was going to commandeer Monica and Chandler's apartment (where the actors seemed to hang in their off time) and just run my parts.

"Excuse me, Jennifer Aniston! Courteney Cox Arquette is about to look at my crotch. This guest star has a ladder and a bucket to rehearse with!"

To prepare, I went over and over the scene in my mind, and really tried to focus during the two rehearsals we had. The first scene went okay when I was out on a balcony and had to come in and talk to Chandler. Mathew Perry was nice and relaxed, and I just remember we chatted about roller coasters. The final scene in the kitchen was the one I was nervous about—I had to dust on the top of Monica and Chandler's cabinets, so I had to stand on their kitchen counter dusting as far as I could reach. I also had to catch Courteney Cox looking at my crotch by looking down and seeing her head poke out between my legs. We went to rehearse, and I tried to pay extra attention to the physical aspects and still be a funny and good scene partner for Courteney.

I was climbing on the crowded counter and was tiptoeing around holding a feather duster in my bootcut jeans and early aughts chunky boots. So far, so good. Courteney was polite, and it seemed to be going well, but I was still intimidated. Earlier that day I panicked in a quiet moment and went into my JJ Myrin mode—when in doubt, compliment. I went on and on about how good Courteney was at physical comedy (which I did think was true, but I sounded like a bit of a weirdo in my praising her).

The second part was when I was supposed to turn around and catch her looking at my crotch. I was coaching myself in my head. *Okay, Arden. You got this. Just look down, make eye contact with*

America's Sweetheart—whose head is between your legs—and continue on with the dialogue. Be a good scene partner. I overthought it, panicked, lost my footing, and accidentally kicked Courteney Cox square in the face.

Watch out, Courteney! I'm about to kick you in the face!

The world stopped and started spinning like I was in *The Matrix*. I could tell that Courteney was deciding whether or not to be cool about the whole affair.

"Oh my god! I'm so sorry! I didn't mean to KICK YOU IN THE FACE, COURTENEY COX."

Silence.

Would she spare me? She could easily have swatted this guest star off the set in the blink of an eye. Did she remember that I had panic-slash-praised her just an hour before?

"Um . . . Don't worry about it. Let's just run it one more time."

Hallelujah! Thank you, Courteney Cox, for giving me the governor's pardon! You will always be my favorite Friend because of this (even though JJ wanted to marry Joey Tribbiani—but that is another story for another day).

The night we filmed in front of the studio audience, I was waiting behind the fake New York City scrim with Sean Penn as the night began. Sean was so sweet and appeared to have some jitters about doing the show. He said his kids loved *Friends*, but he was really nervous about being on it. Of course, he went out and crushed it. He is Sean Freakin' Penn. And thankfully my scene went off without me kicking Courteney in the face a second time.

When the episode aired, they ran an ad with me bending over looking for something under the kitchen sink with my denim-clad ass in the air. Anyone who knows me knows that I did not wear jeans for like fifteen years because I didn't feel comfortable in them. My brother took a photo of my ass and sent it to me.

"Hahahahhaha! Yeah right, like you could fit in Courteney Cox's jeans!" Keeps you grounded.

The years passed, and many wacky neighbor parts later, I got an offer to be on *Grey's Anatomy*. Oh, yes! Not to play a sexy, mysterious new doctor at Grey Sloan Memorial Hospital, but to play a wedding planner—an uptight, Type A, unpleasant wedding planner who is allergic to shellfish and is running the wedding of Alex and Jo at a fancy ranch. The entire cast of *Grey's Anatomy* was in all the scenes that we were doing because it was a big cliffhanger episode.

My character, Kirsten, accidentally eats a piece of shrimp in the middle of the ceremony and goes into anaphylactic shock right before the vows. I plea for an EpiPen, and failing to get one, I collapse onto the ground in front of the entire cast of *Grey's Anatomy*. At first, the doctors try to get a Benadryl into me, but I can't swallow because my throat is closing, so a sea of what appear to be male models decide to save my character another way. (As I have mentioned, I am terrified of doctors, needles, and blood, so I have never watched any episode of any hospital show ever. Lo and behold, the *hottest actors on earth* are cast on the show.)

These hot model doctors decide they're going to have to shove a Benadryl *up my ass*. In front of the entire cast of *Grey's Anatomy*. Alas, their efforts are blocked by the thick, fortress-like knee-length Spanx jammed under the tight shift dress I am wearing. Foiled by my armor-like undergarments, super hunk Alex Williams has to flip me back over as hives and sores spread all over my cleavage and face, and someone decides to do an emergency tracheotomy.

Because they are at an outdoor wedding and not a hospital, they use what is at hand to cut a hole into my windpipe to save my character, using nothing but vodka and a knife. There was nothing handy to keep my windpipe open, so they had to keep my throat open by jamming it with a *decorative child's pinwheel* that spins blood in the wind after it is inserted into my neck. Oh, and to enact this I had to wear a metal rig on my neck—essentially a giant metal neck harness that looked like flesh but meant that I couldn't turn my head and that I needed assistance standing up at the end of the scene.

After we finished the last take of one angle, I was on the ground with a pinwheel in my neck in a tight shift dress, my knee-length Victorian underwear poking out. It was right before

lunch, and it happened to be a crew member's birthday, so
they wheeled out a giant cake and sang happy birthday to her.
Everyone was surrounding me, but I was still on the ground and
starstruck, so I just sang from the ground, and then everyone left
to go to lunch. I was stuck on the ground like a beached seal.
After a few minutes, one of the actors, Matt, noticed that I had
been left behind and came over and gave me a hand.

The pinnacle for me was that the episode was directed by
Debbie Allen. *THE* DEBBIE ALLEN of *Fame*, whom I had
stalked from the TV set of my childhood den! She arrived on set
resplendent in a fur coat and red Ugg boots. Just as elegant as I
imagined she would be when I was a child. I needed to befriend
Debbie and *prove to her* that I had the goods to make it!! My
highlight of the week was when we were doing a walk-through
of the upcoming scene, and I was probably smiling at her like a
starstruck idiot. She looked at me and said, "Act in pain, heffer!"
and walked away. Hallelujah! She did not disappoint!!

Sometimes I try to picture what my high school friends
are doing for work that day and compare it with the unusual
journey I'm having. I am always so delighted and in wonder
of the odd experiences I get to have playing these offbeat
characters. I love my lane of the highway. I think about little
Arden in the fields of Rhode Island wishing upon a star to get
to New York or LA, and I could only have prayed that one
day Debbie Allen would call me a heffer. I loved it. I loved her.
Dreams do come true.

Pigcasso

I submitted the proposal for this book in the winter of 2019. My dream was to sell it, and then when the book came out, go on a book tour and surprise my mom by bringing her along with me on the road. I wanted her to do her own segment during book readings, called "JJ's Corner," where people could ask her advice. My mom LOVED to give advice, whether you asked for it or not.

"You need to whiten your teeth, Barbara!"

"Put a little rouge on it, Donna!"

"How about some bangs, Marjorie? Why not?! Bang it out!"

Me and JJ having a night out before our show in Nashville.

JJ had performed with me once before at a show in Nashville. I was doing a live *Will You Accept This Rose?* podcast with my friend actor Rob Benedict, and I brought her along with us. She had never performed on stage before *in her entire life* (including school plays) and used the mic more like a suggestion than a necessity. She gesticulated with the mic to make her point, but didn't actually speak into it or use it to be amplified. Nevertheless, she *killed* it. The crowd ate her up.

I can see why. She was hilarious that weekend. She had just started dating for the first time in fifty years and wasn't interested in men her own age.

"I don't want to be a nurse or a purse. Have you ever seen old-man balls? Trust me, you don't want to. I don't want to date guys my age. I would date your friend Rob here."

Rob plays God on *Supernatural*, is movie star handsome, forty-five years old, and *in a relationship*. I told Rob that my mom wanted to date him, and without missing a beat, he said, "I would totally date your mom."

I hadn't told my mom about my book tour idea, or even that a book was in the works. I was waiting for the deal to close, and I wanted to surprise her.

I found out that there was an offer for my book at the beginning of March, right when I started season two of *Insatiable*, and I was back in Atlanta for filming. I was so excited—life was a dream. I was hopeful that the book deal would close and was thrilled. I had also just been promoted to a series regular and was so proud and happy to be an official cast member of a show that I loved. We were back in production for four days and I said to one of my coworkers, "It's so much more fun to be here without a newly dead parent!"

I had had a hard time the first season of filming. On the one hand, I was thrilled to play the unapologetic villain on a cool Netflix show, and I adored my boss Lauren Gussis and my coworkers. On the other hand, I was reeling because my dad had passed away right before filming began, and I was stunned at how much grief I had. I felt isolated processing Willy's death in an Airbnb in Atlanta, for five months and three thousand miles from my family and friends.

Season two was supposed to be a fresh start. I was feeling more like myself and really wanted to dive in and get to know my castmates more. During the first episode, the spectacular Debby Ryan organized a group outing to take a Twerkout Workout and asked if I wanted to join. Obviously, I was *in*. I mean what kind of a monster do you think I am? I headed down to the twerkout ready to go. I was intrigued when I arrived because it took place in a rec center in a Hasidic development. Seemed like an odd spot for the class, but that just made me more curious about what was going to unfold. A few of the people from the show were already there. We were all dressed up and ready to learn how to twerk!

The instructor was late and my phone rang. It was my mom's business partner, Lisa.

"Have you talked to your mom?"

"No. Why? Is something wrong?"

"No. It's just that she's working on a closing and a few people haven't been able to get in touch with her for a couple of days."

I didn't want to get roped into this. The previous winter I had gotten yelled at by my mom when one night I couldn't get in touch with her for hours. It was not like JJ—this was a lady who *loved* to chat on the phone. I was concerned because once my dad had passed away, I didn't like the idea of her living alone in the country in the middle of a field. She never owned a key for the front door and didn't lock any windows or doors. My brother and I had begged her to at least lock the doors at night. I knew her "attack kitty" Mittens wouldn't scare anyone off. When I couldn't get in touch with her, I eventually called the Little Compton Police Department, which sent an officer to check on her. She wasn't home. My mind started reeling, and I was worried she had gotten into some kind of car accident.

The night I called the cops it turned out that she had stayed out late at a dinner party and left her cell phone in her purse in the closet, so she missed all my calls. Here she was: living her best life, starting to come out of the cocoon of grief after my dad's illness and death, and I was the weird overprotective daughter. When she finally did get home, she was mortified that the cops had showed up and was angry with me.

"But what if something happened to you? You are all by yourself there. I don't want you to be on the floor for a few days and no one knows."

"What is wrong with you? Are you on something? You're crazy if you think anything is going to happen to me. You are stuck with me until I am a hundred and ten."

So when Lisa called me, I really didn't want anything to do with it.

"She's probably at the movies or having dinner with a girlfriend. I'm sure she's fine."

We called my brother, who also had not talked to her. We decided it was best if Lisa just drove over to JJ's house. Lisa got there, and lo and behold the door was actually locked. I never thought my mom would listen to me about that, but she had. Lisa walked around the outside of the house and looked in all the windows while we were on the phone with her and didn't see my mom. She did see my mom's purse in the kitchen. She got a ladder and was able to look in the garage and saw that my mom's car was still there.

As I was learning all of this, the Twerkout instructor arrived thirty minutes late with a light-up boom box and two pitchers of margaritas. She was busy fighting with the people at the rec center who said she was using the space illegally and that they had told her to stop holding her classes there.

Everyone started the class without me. As most of my friends were learning how to twerk, I was pacing around in the hall outside the rec room, and Debby waited with me.

Alarik and I were on the phone with Lisa when she eventually got into the house. She walked back toward my mom's bedroom and we just heard her say, "Oh my god. I need to call the police."

And then she hung up.

Holy. Shit. WHAT DO YOU MEAN YOU NEED TO CALL THE POLICE!!?? Alarik and I tried to keep calm, but we were both starting to panic. No one wants to hear that. My mind was reeling. We called Lisa back.

"Hi."

"Hi."

"Is she dead?"

SILENCE.

"Yes. I'm so sorry. I think she's been here for a few days."

My worst fear had materialized. My poor, sweet mom had been on the floor for a few days. And we didn't know. Life went on as usual, and that poor angel was on the floor. I will forever be grateful to Lisa for calling me, for caring enough to wonder where my mom was and for going to look for her. Here's to small towns and how much people look after one another!

I never did learn how to twerk.

Debby drove me back to my Airbnb. And in that moment, I realized something odd. I had never seen Debby behind the wheel before.

"Just so you know, I *do* have a license. You may never have seen me do this before, but I actually do know how to drive."

Debby watched me leave my body and make weird jokes to people on the phone. I had to talk to the police officer who had to go to the house. Debby heard me lie to him about my age and try to make light of the situation.

"My age? Well I CAN play thirty-four with the right lighting."

"Well, officer, it's just as she would have always wanted it, for me to find out about her death at a Twerkout class in a Hasidic rec center."

We got to my Airbnb. I was floating above my body like a Macy's Day Parade balloon whose handlers had lost control of it. I had just gotten a weighted blanket to help me with anxiety, and before Debby left I insisted that she try it and captured her under its web.

Before she left, I told Debby that I had heard the number one regulator of trauma is to play. Any kind of play—dancing, games, cartwheels, singing, crafting, whatever. Later that night, Debby texted me a Spotify playlist in honor of JJ—for me and my brother to dance to.

Debby passed me off to my husband, Dan, who happened to be visiting me in Atlanta for the weekend. Dan and my mom loved each other and were a team. He used to take her on little dates in New York when we lived there and she would come visit. They would go to the Muppets exhibit or the butterfly show at the American Museum of Natural History and get hot cocoas afterward. I had never seen Dan cry before, but when he called his parents to tell them what happened, he broke down and made a sound I had never heard before or since. Like a hurt animal.

We hopped on a plane to Providence and steeled ourselves for the weekend. When Dan, my brother, his wife, and I walked into my childhood home, it was so odd—like a life interrupted. My mom's little puffy white coat was still on the back of her chair in the kitchen. There was toast in the toaster and tea in her cup. She died making her favorite meal—toast. It was as if she was going to walk through the door at any moment, so happy that we were all there. I could just hear her say, "Oh, good, all my chickens are in one basket!"

How could she just be gone? Vanished?

It was the oddest thing—even though her death was sudden and unexpected, the list maker JJ Myrin had left little clues around the house from the great beyond for us. There was a map in the hallway all wrapped up with a note taped to it, addressed to me and my brother.

ARDEN AND ALARIK: THIS MAP IS VALUABLE. DO NOT THROW AWAY. TAKE IT TO AN ANTIQUE DEALER AND TRY TO SELL IT.

WTF?? Notes like this were all over the house. Even in death my mom was helpful and organized.

We quickly had to plan a funeral and a memorial lunch, and we wanted to have photos on foam core boards of my mom at all ages with her friends, for people to enjoy. Lo and behold, stacked neatly on her bedside table was a stack of copies of fun vintage photos of my mom with her family and friends—photos I had never seen before—duplicated, curated and organized, and waiting to be assembled on a board. My old bed was even covered in glue sticks and glue guns just waiting for a craft project. This was not the craft we wanted to make. Alarik's wife was freaked out by all of it.

"She KNEW she was dying and didn't tell us!"

But I am the Nancy Drew of JJ. I found some paint samples and quickly sleuthed what she had been doing—decluttering and redecorating. When in doubt, get a new throw pillow and make a salon wall of family photos! JJ was starting a new chapter after my dad died and wanted to have a fresh start. I knew she'd read the Marie Kondo book about the magic of tidying up, because she made everyone in her life read it.

"How are you going to thrive, Sandra, if your house is filled with CLUTTER? Get rid of it!"

I suspect the map she set aside for me and my brother didn't spark joy, but ever the Yankee, she wanted money for it.

We had to find a place to hold the funeral. Little Compton has very few public spaces, and my family did not go to church. We put our hats in our hand and asked the local church for a favor, to see if we could hold her funeral there. They kindly (and possibly reluctantly) agreed. Alarik and I met with the young, cool Reverend Rachel, who was so gracious. I almost blew it when I asked if we could play music during the service.

"Of course, you can play music."

"Would it be okay if we played 'All the Single Ladies' by Beyoncé? It was her favorite song."

Silence.

"Ummmmm . . . NO. No, that would not be okay."

When we got to Rhode Island we found an Alexa Echo that Alarik had given to JJ for Christmas. It was in her "to be regifted" basket. We dusted it off and played Debby's playlist all week as we cried, crafted, and made arrangements. JJ loved a good trip to Michaels, the arts and crafts store, so we decided to follow in her footsteps and make something to give to everyone who came to her funeral. She had been in the process of readying her field to replace all the hay with wildflowers.

My sister-in-law had the genius idea to make little burlap bags filled with wildflower seeds and sealed with a glitter "J" to hand out to people to plant their own JJ tribute wildflower garden. Alarik, Sheryle, Katie, Andrew, Alarik's wife, Dan, Mittens, and I stayed up for two days straight cutting, gluing, glittering, and filling bags with seeds, or, as we called it, grief-crafting. It is the one and only time I have ever seen my brother use a glue gun. JJ would have been so happy.

Dancing to the playlist helped get us through the unimaginable—we danced and crafted to Katy Perry (obviously), ABBA, Beyoncé, Bruno Mars, and more. We danced to "Dancing Queen," and then my brother screamed, "Thank you, Debby Ryan!" and we lay on the floor and cried.

The morning of the funeral, Alarik and I were in the

JJ's tribute wildflower bags. The one and only time I have ever seen my brother use a glue gun.

house trying to prep ourselves for the incomprehensible. We were starting to freak out, concerned that we would not be able to pull ourselves together to be in public. Suddenly, and completely out of the blue, JJ's Alexa Echo woke up and started talking to us.

"Hello."

Alarik and I looked at each other.

"Did you hear that?"

Alexa barreled through

"It's 9:05 a.m. It is fifty-seven degrees. In the news today, a pig in South Africa has taught itself to paint. They are calling it Pigcasso. Pigcasso's paintings regularly sell for between four and five thousand dollars, and that is what is in the news today."

Pig-fucking-casso.

Whatever you believe in, Alarik and I both felt like JJ was talking to us through Alexa with the most *insane headline ever* to tell us to smile and get ourselves together. We decided it was time to JJ up! So we did. Alarik, Pigcasso, and I got on with it, and we held our heads high, even though our hearts were broken. On my way to the funeral I found out that my book deal closed. The e-mail read:

HOPE YOU'RE HAVING A GREAT WEEK! WE ARE SO EXCITED TO DO THIS BOOK WITH YOU.

Life is loco in the coco. It was a beautiful, horrible day. Little Compton was wonderful and loving and wrapped its arms around us. We cried and hugged and laughed and I took a nap on the floor in the middle of our living room in a crowd of people.

The next day, Dan flew me and Mittens[25] back to Atlanta—I still had a full season of *Insatiable* to shoot—and then he headed back to LA for work. I was alone again in an Atlanta Airbnb, with another deceased parent, a cat with four "thumbs," and ten episodes to film. I had to channel my inner JJ, who told me that work is good for the soul.

---

25. Did you think I was just gonna leave behind the little kitty with FOUR extra "thumbs"? Think again. That cat was coming with ME.

When I got back to the set of *Insatiable*, everyone was so kind. I absolutely love this show. But the universe has a sick sense of humor. The scene we were filming my first day back? A funeral scene.

How the hell did my fun little beach book I was supposed to write all of a sudden become *Four Funerals and a Wedding*!?!

All day, people in the scene were singing a comic song called "Dead Girl."

I have never done major drugs, but I sort of felt like I was tripping. Everyone knew how weird it was to be doing this fake funeral two days after I had my mom's real funeral (and a year after I had my dad's funeral). People gave me hugs and apologized. I asked sweet Michael Provost, who plays Brick on the show, "What do you think of all this?" And he said, "It's nuts."

It got even weirder. On the show I played Regina Sinclair, the number two realtor, whose slogan is "Number Two and Loving It!" That first day back, a notary public had to come to my trailer for me to sign my mom's will, at which point I inherited my mom's share of Little Compton Real Estate, and so I really *was* officially the number two real estate agent in Little Compton—but not really loving it. I burst into tears, and the notary public gave me a huge hug, slipped me her card, and told me she could hook me up with some black-market Xanax.

Yesterday marks one month since I found out that my mom passed away, and I still get cards and flowers and e-mails every day. I am overwhelmed and so hopeful by this display of human tenderness.

And then the most wonderful thing happened. It was a Sunday, and I had many enticing offers and was so grateful for that. But I said no to all of them. Because I had to write. I had to write *this book*. And I was procrastinating, but I do that (even when I am not grieving). On the best of days, I dillydally and do my laundry and take naps and clean my apartment. So I was home, and I was feeling like I should have been doing something fun. Something social. *Anything* other than sitting around, avoiding writing, when all my pals were off living their lives.

Me and my BFFATL Debby. I love her and am so grateful she is my friend.

When I got a text from teen dream heartthrob Michael Provost asking if I was home, I was happy to say that I was. Clearly, this was a sign from the universe that I was supposed to socialize and *not write*. Ten minutes later I opened the door to find one of the sweetest things that I have ever seen.

Standing on my doorstep was Michael holding a homemade lasagna. *A homemade lasagna. That he had made.* On his Saturday night. Twenty-one-year-old Michael, who was now legal and could have gone out on the town, had stayed in his house, watched a YouTube tutorial on "How to Make a Lasagna," and proceeded to make his grieving adult lady coworker a lasagna. Is that not the sweetest thing you have *ever heard*?

He said, "I didn't know what to say to you the day you came back from your mom's funeral. You asked me what I thought and I didn't have the right words. I have never been through something like this. So, I have been thinking about it a lot, and I remembered that when I was growing up and someone my family knew died, my mom would make their family a lasagna. So, I made you a lasagna."

America's sweetheart Michael Provost with the homemade lasagna he made for me.

There is goodness in the world.

I have done many jobs since I made it outta Little Compton, but I think *Insatiable* would have been my favorite anyway. You can knock Regina down, but you can't take her out. Because she is resilient. And so am I. But beyond that, I don't know why each filming season I lost a parent and immediately got thrown into an Airbnb in Atlanta, away from my regular life and my husband and family and friends. But having this happen a second time makes me believe there are no accidents.

In a weird way, I think being in Atlanta gave me the privacy to have a conversation with myself, with JJ, and with my grief that I might have distracted myself from had I been at home. I go on walks, I see the beautiful flowers blooming, I talk to JJ, I go to work, I talk to my mom here on the page, I cry and nap under my weighted blanket. And lo and behold, I did make friends. Real friends.

The world embraced me. Sarah Colonna would cat-sit Mittens when I was working and she wasn't. Debby and I became really tight—she is a beautiful, bright light who really showed up for me when my world blew apart. I never would have guessed that a twenty-five-year-old former Disney star would be my BFF in Atlanta, but I have learned not to make predictions about life. We have played and

Me and Kimmy vintage shopping on Easter.

laughed, and she keeps trying to get me to rock streetwear.

Kimmy Shields spent Easter with me shopping for vintage clothes on a day that was my mom's favorite holiday. I have giggled at dinners for hours with our director, Andy Flemming, and our showrunner, Lauren. People socialized with me even when I was (and still am) not at my best.

I asked the very wise, very intuitive Lauren for her thoughts. She had met my mom and loved her, too. She told me, "I just see butterflies. Lots and lots of butterflies for you. You will make something from this."

I think this book is my batch of butterflies.

I hope one of the takeaways of my mom's death is that I can release worry. My biggest fear had happened—my mom died and had been alone on the floor for three days, but worrying about it didn't prevent it, and it didn't spare me the grief when it happened. As a perpetual worrywart, I truly hope I can see the futility of living life in fear of what can happen.

I am here to tell you that you can survive your biggest fear and still be okay, and still fundamentally be yourself. I am grieving, and I am in pain, but I will be okay. I know I have to feel it to heal it. I will miss my mom every day of my life—but JJ did not raise a drip!

God forbid something like this happens to you, here's what I'm doing that seems to be working for me—my Grief Island Recipe Part 2 as it were.

Schedule time to cry (which is not to say you aren't free to cry as often as you need to). But for me, I can tend to push things down and efficiently dive back into the to-do list of my life, and that's not really facing things. There are all sorts of helpers out there—friends, family, therapists, et cetera.

Find a place where you can go a few times a week and just be not okay and face the fact that you are grieving. I found a really nice therapist in Atlanta who has been so helpful. Knowing I am going to get to exhale and be not okay a few times a week in a therapist's office makes it much easier for me to keep it together when I need to (like at work). I know therapists can be pricey, but there are loads of affordable, wonderful grief and twelve-step groups out there.

I also schedule time to play—as I mentioned earlier, I heard somewhere that to play is the number one regulator of trauma. I don't know whether this is true or not, but testing it out with my brother these last few weeks seems to be working for us. Dancing (even around your house) is great. For the past four weeks, I have danced, gone to karaoke, and been to my first roller derby. Debby dragged me on scooters around Piedmont Park (and I actually enjoyed it), and I have eaten more tacos with friends in the past four weeks than I have in my entire life. Apparently, the grief Mom-sized hole in my heart needs TACOS.

I allow myself to cancel. Obviously, you have to show up for work, but beyond that, I understand that I am more tired and a little crazier than normal, and if I show up somewhere and I am just not up for it, I allow myself to leave. Or cancel before I go.

NAPS. Oh, naps are heaven. If possible, naps with a weighted blanket and a kitty cat. A tiny two-year-old kitty with thumbs and giant paws the size of Kareem Abdul-Jabbar's hands makes for the best nurse!

Exercise. I take workout classes and allow myself to be twenty minutes late to all of them. I really have lowered the bar and am sort of having a "better late than never" approach to life right now (except for work—don't be late to work, bunnies!). Walks are good, too. Slow shuffles give me fresh air and the chance to look at nature, talk to my mom, and sometimes cry in public (but I keep it moving so I don't freak out Atlanta! JJ didn't raise no public crying drip).

As I mentioned before, don't underestimate the power of reality TV! *The Great British Bake Off* and *Queer Eye* are both great choices in place of (or in addition to) prescription drugs.

Some people want you to grieve faster than you will. To those people I say, "Thanks for playing! BYEEEEE!" I know they mean well, and I don't take it personally, but a person who

I love very much is gone, and it is perfectly appropriate to feel sad for a while. Probably for a very long time to come. Allow yourself time to grieve.

Work. Work is important, not just for keeping the electric company from shutting your lights off, but to get outside of yourself a few hours every day. To give yourself a distraction, a task, some self-esteem, and a paycheck.

One of the many JJ tribute wildflower gardens from the seeds we gave out at her funeral.

Oh, and of course, watch the Katy Perry documentary.

When my mom died, I thought, *You have got to be fucking kidding me. Again??* I have had many people tell me how sorry they are that I can't just go collapse at home, but I truly believe this is where I am supposed to be. And writing this book has actually felt like having a conversation with my mom.

When I left Little Compton to make my mark all those years ago, there were many things I didn't know how to do or wasn't sure about in this world, but the truth is that everything wonderful, magical, and adventurous in the way I was taught to navigate life started back in that town of three thousand people.

In a small house in the country. Because of a dare with the magical wizard herself, JJ.

I am so proud to be Little Miss Little Compton. I miss you, JJ. I love you. And I'll see you on the other side with a glue gun, some glitter, and an Isaac Mizrahi blouse.

EPILOGUE

It is now July 2019. We couldn't get JJ cremated in time for the funeral because there was a holdup with the horrible paperwork of death. Alarik and I made our journey to Little Compton to get JJ's ashes last week and put most of them in a sassy Jonathan Adler–style urn, which she would have loved. We buried her next to her truth-or-dare love of her life, Willy.

But we saved a few of the ashes. JJ's friend had passed away a few years ago and planned her own funeral in which her ashes were shot off with fireworks. My mom was wowed by the idea.

I'm not saying we did this (because it may not be legal), but perhaps we had a small gathering with a few of her closest girlfriends, played "All the Single Ladies," and lit up some giant sparklers of our own. And maybe Adolf went up to New Hampshire to purchase fireworks to fill with a little bit of JJ's ashes in them.

We may or may not have lit them off in her yard, over her field. Dan is a veteran of the Air Force and he said it reminded him of a sparkly version of a twenty-one gun salute. It was beautiful and festive and full of light. And then the strangest thing happened.

JJ's hay field lit up, bursting with fireflies, hundreds and hundreds of fireflies, like she was winking at us from the afterlife. I think she was happy to be home and was reminding us to put a little razzle-dazzle into everything we do while we are still here on earth. I think of it like the great beyond version of jazz hands, as JJ made her way to her next big adventure in the sky. Hey, Lauren, turns out it was a combination of butterflies *and* fireflies—and, of course, raising her kids to not be drips.

ACKNOWLEDGMENTS

I would love to thank:

The town of Little Compton, Rhode Island, for shaping me into the human that I am. I feel so lucky to have grown up there and am so grateful for the kindness you have all displayed to me and my brother during the last few years.

My brother, Alarik, who is the BEST. I wouldn't be who I am without having you as a bro. Thanks for introducing me to Steve Martin, Monty Python, and Mel Brooks.

Sheryle and Katie for being my partners in crime and for allowing me to write about our misadventures. I love you both!

My friends Jacob Mesczaros, Bruce McKoy, Samantha Dunn, Lisa DeLarios, and Anna Hossnieh, who read early drafts of this book and gave me notes along the way.

Sweet Debby Ryan for writing my beautiful foreword. I love it, I love you, and am so grateful you are my friend. You are my sparkly sister from another mister. P.S. I think you dated the right drummer.

Thank you to Chelsea Handler for the lovely quote and for having me on *Chelsea Lately* all those years.

Thank you to Amy Schumer for so generously giving me a beautiful quote and for being such a fearless comedic inspiration to so many women.

Miss Molly Shannon, you are such a beautiful human and a brave comedic performer. You and Gilda are tied for #1 *SNL* All-Stars to me. Thank you for the quote.

To Amy, Chelsea, and Molly: If you can't see it you can't be it. And you all help me see it.

Thank you to Robyn Von Swank for taking such a badass picture for the cover and my friend Rebekkah Drake for taking the lovely author photo of me. I love you so much and am so glad you are my friend. And thank you, Cassy Meiers, for getting me camera ready.

All of the people who encouraged me, read drafts, gave me quotes, and gave me a nudge along the way: Cris and Stella McCall, Rob Cohen, Jill Leiderman, Sara Benincasa, Amy Guglielmo, Michael Provost, Julie Anne Robinson, Adam Griffin and Diandra Younesi, Erin Foley, Lauren Lapkus, Bryan Safi, Jordan Rawlins, and Zach Galifianakis.

The best book agent ever, Robert Guinsler at Sterling Lord Literistic. Thank you for hunting me down! You are hilarious and such a hard worker. I feel so lucky to have you as my agent. And thank you, Sarah Colonna, for hooking us up.

Thanks to my podcast peeps and listeners for walking through the fire with me these last few years, and all the good people on *Insatiable* for wrapping your arms around me two years in a row.

My editor Jordana Hawkins, my copy editor Michael McConnell, and everyone at Running Press and Hachette for helping me shape this book, and the opportunity to share my unusual upbringing with the world. I am so thankful for all your notes and that you believed in my voice.

Lauren Hom for the gorgeous custom lettering and illustrations on the cover of the book, and Rachel Peckman for the book design.

To my publicist, Whitney Tancred, for helping me sell this sucker! You rock!

And to Dan, thank you for being my rock. I love you so much.